Pickles, Peaches & Chocolate

...easy, elegant gifts from your kitchen

by Karen Ward

Pickles, Peaches & Chocolate
...easy and elegant gifts from your kitchen

Design: Creative Fusion
Food Stylist: Karen Ward
Photography: Ron Bez

Published by: C & K Enterprises
P.O. Box 9005-508
La Mesa, CA, 91944-9005

First Edition, May 1999

ISBN 0-9666580-0-0
Library of Congress Catalog Card Number: 98-91753

Printed in the USA by
WIMMER
The Wimmer Companies
Memphis
1-800-548-2537

Acknowledgements

To my friends and family. Your support, good wishes, and belief in this project helped me make my dream a reality. I hope you enjoy it as much as I enjoyed putting it together.

To Chris, my husband and toughest critic. Your comments, support and advice have kept me going.

To George and Martha, my parents. Your encouragement and outlook on life has been invaluable.

To Diana, my sister and project supporter, who told me to "get on with it". You helped me keep my wits about me with your guidance and insight. You are truly an inspiration, I know no other quite like you.

To Judy, my "best bud" and gardening pal. How could I get along without you and your garden? The unlimited variety and abundance of the harvest lets me experiment to my heart's content.

To "The Tasters", who are many. Thanks for your patience in sampling "the experiments" as well as trying "just one more thing".

To "The Recipe Contributors". Thanks for parting with your favorites so that they may be shared and enjoyed by others.

To Ron Bez, an incredible photographer and individual. Your unrelenting drive for "the best shot" made my food come to life.

To Christy, Michelle, and Creative Fusion. Thanks for keeping me focused and on track while bringing order to my work.

To Lisa Curtis, Belle Long, and John Sandoval. Special thanks for your assistance in my project development.

Cover Photographs:
Sweet Pickle Chips
Pickled Peaches
Karen's Macadamia Nut Fudge

Pickles, Peaches & Chocolate

...easy, elegant gifts from your kitchen

Before the Gift

Gifts come in all shapes and sizes. For as long as I can remember, I have been a gift-giver. Anything would do... from one of those "interesting" clay creations from art class in school (the one Mother always loved and never asked "what is it?") to a rock wrapped in a scrap of fabric, or a cookie.

Regardless of the gift, something from your home or kitchen is a wonderful, thoughtful way to tell someone how much you care about them. Whether you are an experienced creator of tasty treats, or a newcomer to the kitchen, these easy recipes can make you look like a pro in no time.

The recipes have been sorted by the amount of cooking required to prepare the gift (no cooking, some cooking, lot'sa cooking). Preparation times have purposely been omitted as everyone operates at their own speed. With a little bit of thought and creativity, it's easy to impress and impossible to resist taste-testing.

Here are some ideas to help you get going.....

- Develop a plan! I know this is a four-letter word, but planning ahead can save you time, money, and eliminate frustration.

- Write your plan down and remember to read it. Cross things off as you complete them.

- Prepare items within the scope of the time you have. Your gift will not be appreciated **more** if you make it in the middle of the night!

- Diversify your choices when planning. Utilize the chapter headings (no, some, or lot'sa cooking) to create quick gifts or more time-consuming ones.

- Develop a theme and carry it throughout the gift presentation. This can be anything from a color to a theme of chile peppers or flowers.

- Reflect something of yourself in the gifts you create and give. This could be a hand-made note tag with a special message inside or a "package topper" of a favorite kitchen tool.

- Include the recipe and instructions for preparation with the gift.

- Always, always, always read a recipe all of the way through before attempting to make it.

- Make sure you have all of the ingredients on hand. Nothing is more frustrating than starting to make something and realizing you need to drop everything and go to the store.

  And finally, remember to keep things simple, enjoy yourself, and have fun!

Gift Packaging Thoughts

*Packaging allows you to express yourself. Let only your imagination be
your creative limitation. Let's say your best friend says, "I really want a
plain white casserole dish for my birthday." You think, "How boring
and unexciting!" Well, don't just hand them the gift, fill it up!*

*Each recipe has a specific suggestion for gift-giving, but here are a few
more ideas:*

Casserole Dish - fill with the ingredients for ***"Potatoes Romanoff"***
or ***"Simply, Rice Dish"***; or prepare the ingredients to the point of
final baking in the "gift casserole dish", cover tightly with plastic
wrap, add cellophane, a bow, and a kitchen utensil, such as wooden
spoon or a rubber scraper.

Crock Pot - give the ingredients for ***"Calico Beans"***. No
excuses for not using this appliance right away! Oops, too many
products to fit in the crock pot? Put all of the items in a
large basket or just fill a gift bag with the overflow items.

Muffin Pan - bake a dozen of the ***"Six Week Bran Muffins"***. Wrap
each muffin in colored plastic wrap, place in the muffin pan and
instant gift! You could also include the leftover batter in a
measuring cup.

Storage Containers - Select container sizes to stack
proportionately on top of each other. Fill each container with
something different, stack them, and tie together with ribbon.
Combination ideas: ***"Spiced Whole Almonds"***, ***"Chocolate Dipped
Pretzels"***, and ***"Spiced Tea Mix"*** or a variety of ***"Pesto Pastes"*** and
a container of ***"Pocket Bread Toast Triangles"***.

Gift wrapping ideas exist everywhere. Look around and you'll be amazed at what you find. Use items that can be re-used. A few ideas....canning jars, brown paper bags, berry boxes, plates, flower pots or mixing bowls. *"The Best Homemade Croutons"* look great in a glass measuring cup or a crystal candy jar.

Here are some everyday items you may have overlooked for gift packaging:

- sewing notions in place of ribbon: rick rack, satin ribbon, bias tape, lace, eyelet.
- ribbon to reflect your theme: plaid, gingham, floral.
- gift tag alternatives: price tags or inventory style tags available at office supply stores.
- flower pots or vases filled with bags of goodies.
- colored pipe cleaners for twist ties and bows.
- brown or white paper bags decorated with dried flowers and raffia.
- utility twine, sisal, even small diameter rope in place of ribbon. Look for colored varieties.
- a waste basket (new and unused, of course) in place of a basket or gift bag.
- decorate tags, plain wrapping paper, or paper bags with rubber stamps, stickers, colored marking pens, or crayons too.

Now that you're filled with ideas, let's get started!

No Cooking

Easy gifts with little clean-up! These recipes require no cooking to prepare them for consumption or gift-giving...and boiling water doesn't count as cooking.

Thirst Quenchers:
Chocolate Espresso Mix
Dried Fruit Liqueur
Irish Creme Liqueur
Karen's Coffee Liqueur
Mulling Spices
Spiced Tea Mix
Chris Ward's Transfusions

Dips & Doodles:
Holly Wreath Spread
Macadamia Nut Hummus
Many Layer Dip
Overnight Guacamole Taco Dip
Sun-Dried Tomato Torte
Nine Bean Soup Mix
About Seasonings and Spices
- Cajun Spice
- Curry Powder
- Herbs of Provence
- Italian Herb Seasoning

On Top & Around:
About Pesto Paste
- Basic Pesto Paste
- Not-So-Rich Pesto Paste
- Macadamia Nut Pesto Paste
- Red Basil Pesto Paste
- Roasted Pepper Pesto Paste
- Sun-Dried Tomato Pesto Paste

About Salad Dressing
- Balsamic Vinaigrette
- Mustard Dressing
- Chive-Mustard Dressing
- Fruit Vinaigrette
- Chinese Black Bean
  Vinaigrette
- My Dressing
- Papaya Seed Salad Dressing
- Pesto Paste Salad Dressing
- Vinaigrette Dressing

In Addition To:
Coffee Liqueur Honey Butter
About Raw Salsas
- Cilantro Salsa
- Mango Salsa
- Papaya Salsa
Aloha Marinade
Flank Steak Marinade
Spicy Soy Sauce

After It's Over:
"For-A-Group" Chocolate Eclair

Chocolate Espresso Mix

Makes 2 cups

Serve steaming hot with a cinnamon stick for stirring. Great!

1 cup granulated sugar
2/3 cup unsweetened cocoa
1-1/2 teaspoons ground cinnamon
1/2 teaspoon ground nutmeg
2 tablespoons instant espresso powder
1/2 cup nonfat dry milk

1. Combine all ingredients and stir to mix.

2. Store in an airtight container until ready to use or make individual packages for gift giving.

   For serving: Combine 3/4 cup hot milk with 3 tablespoons of dry mix. (Adjust the amount of mix to achieve the flavor of your liking.) Stir until mix is dissolved. Garnish with whipped cream or marshmallows and a cinnamon stick.

   Note: *To make more than one cup at a time, heat milk in a saucepan over medium heat. When the milk is hot, add the dry mix and stir with a whisk. Heat until steaming, but do not boil.*

This is great packaged in anything from decorative tins to cellophane bags stuffed into a coffee mug. Garnish the package with some cinnamon sticks for "swizzle-ing".

Dried Fruit Liqueur

Makes 4 quarts

When making this in smaller containers, use different fruits or make your own "mixed fruit medley".

1 pound dried fruit, whole or pieces
1 bottle (750 ml) sweet white wine
1 quart brandy
1 quart water
1 (3 inch) cinnamon stick

1. Place fruit into a one gallon container or several smaller ones. If your containers are different sizes, divide the fruit proportionately.

2. Mix wine, brandy, and water together. Pour liquid over the fruit. Add the cinnamon stick, breaking into pieces if using several containers.

3. Let the containers sit at room temperature for at least one month. Gently turn the containers over a few times each week to help the flavors blend.

   Serve over ice cream or in individual brandy glasses with the fruit pieces.

To capture the spectacular colored fruit, a clear jar or wide-mouth bottle is a must. Finish with a raffia wrap and bow.

Irish Creme Liqueur

Makes 1 generous quart

This is wickedly indulgent. Add to coffee, as an ice cream topping, or just all by itself.

1-3/4 cups brandy
1 (14 ounce) can sweetened condensed milk
1/2 pint heavy whipping cream
2 tablespoons chocolate syrup
2 teaspoons instant coffee powder or crystals
1 teaspoon vanilla extract
1/2 teaspoon almond extract

1. Mix all ingredients in a blender until smooth. Place into a container with a tight fitting lid. Store in the refrigerator.

Keeps about one month (if it lasts that long!).

Present in recycled wine bottles and wrap in aluminum foil, shiny side out. Press foil over bottle for a smooth, yet wrinkly look. Add a gingham bow and you're ready to go!

Karen's Coffee Liqueur

Makes 1 gallon

I started making this in college. It fit into my budget and was always well received.

2 cups instant coffee powder or crystals
7 cups granulated sugar
4 cups boiling water
1 quart vodka
1 whole vanilla bean, split

1. Combine coffee powder and sugar in a heatproof bowl. Pour boiling water into the mixture. Stir to dissolve; let cool completely. Add vodka and stir.

2. Place vanilla bean into a one gallon bottle or jug. Add the coffee mixture and seal the bottle. Allow mixture to stand in a dark place for 3 to 4 weeks. This is a must in order to allow the flavors to blend.

    Serve in liqueur glasses, over ice, with cream or milk, or add to coffee.

    Note: *The liqueur may thicken the longer it is allowed to sit, but this in no way affects the product.*

Gift Giving

To bring out the richness of the liqueur, package in a brown colored bottle. If a colored bottle is unavailable, splurge for one that is engraved or has a uniquely embossed design. To finish, tie on an extra long cinnamon stick and some dried flowers.

Mulling Spices

Don't let the costly juniper berries deter you from trying this. Whether creating a spiced wine or cider, the aroma is magnificent. The used packet may be simmered in water to captivate all of the fragrance presented in this aromatic blend.

1 package cheesecloth
6 (6 inch) lengths of poultry twine or string
12 (3 inch) cinnamon sticks, broken into pieces
1/4 cup allspice berries
1/4 cup juniper berries
1/4 cup whole cloves
1 tablespoon ground nutmeg
1 tablespoon ground cardamom
zest of 1 lemon, cut into thin strips
zest of 1 orange, cut into thin strips

1. Cut six 6-inch squares from the cheesecloth. (If cheesecloth is loosely woven, double or triple the cloth). Lay the cheesecloth squares flat.

2. Combine cinnamon sticks, berries, cloves, nutmeg, cardamom, and fruit zest in a mixing bowl. Stir to blend.

3. Divide mix equally between the cheesecloth squares. Tie the bags tightly with the string pieces. Leave the string ends long so that the bag may be easily retrieved from the pot.

    Variation: *For a sweeter spice, add 1 cup dark brown sugar to the above ingredients.*

Preparation Instructions to Include with Mulling Spices:

Place 1 quart cider (or wine) and bag of mulling spices into a saucepan. Heat over medium heat, but do not boil. When the liquid is steaming and aromatic, serve in coffee mugs.

Place the cheesecloth bag in anything from a colored cellophane bag to a tapestry bag. Use as a package topper or tie around the neck of a bottle of wine or cider.

Spiced Tea Mix

Makes 3-1/4 cups

Prepare this one cup at a time to make yourself (or someone else) feel extra special.

2/3 cup instant tea mix, unsweetened
9 ounces orange flavored drink mix
3 ounces lemonade drink mix
1 cup granulated sugar
1 teaspoon ground cinnamon
1/2 teaspoon ground cloves
1/8 teaspoon ground allspice
1/8 teaspoon ground nutmeg

1. Combine all ingredients in a mixing bowl. Store in airtight container until ready to use, or place in smaller containers for giving.

Preparation Instructions to Include with Mix:

Add 1 tablespoon of mix to 6 ounces of boiling water. Adjust the flavor for personal preference.

Package in anything from a plastic airtight container to a decorative tin to a glass canning jar. If you've found that extra-special mug or teacup, tie a brightly colored ribbon on a baggie of mix and place it in the cup.

Chris Ward's Transfusions

Makes 1 gallon

This uniquely seasoned Bloody Mary was adapted from the tasty concoction served in the Windsock Lounge at the now non-existent Ka'anapali Airport. This is my husband's tribute to "High School Harry", the creator of this world class beverage.

26 ounces sweet and sour mix
7 ounces Worcestershire sauce
1 teaspoon Tabasco sauce
2 ounces bottled lime juice
2 ounces caraway seed liqueur (such as Aquavit)
2 tablespoons celery salt
2 tablespoons dried dill weed
1 teaspoon seasoned pepper
2 (46 ounce) cans tomato juice

1. Combine all ingredients in a 4-quart mixing container. Shake well. Refrigerate at least 24 hours to allow the flavors to blend.

   To serve, pour over ice. Vodka and a stalk of celery may be added.

Gift Giving

The only deciding factor in packaging this gift is the size of the bottle. A quart is just a tease, a half gallon satisfies the taste buds, but do you really want to part with the whole gallon? If you feel the need to add something to the gift, include some glass swizzle sticks.

Holly Wreath Spread

Makes 2-1/2 cups

This makes a generous portion and can be made up to two days in advance.

2 (8 ounce) packages cream cheese, at room temperature
1/2 cup Miracle Whip-style salad dressing
1/3 cup grated Parmesan cheese
6 slices bacon, well-done, drained, and crumbled
2 slices ham, finely chopped
1/3 cup finely chopped green or red bell pepper
1/3 cup finely chopped green onions (including tops)
fresh curly leaf parsley, for garnish
1 (2 ounce) jar pimientos, for garnish
crackers for serving

1. Combine cream cheese, salad dressing, and Parmesan cheese. After well blended, add bacon, ham, bell pepper, and green onions. Stir until all ingredients are blended. Chill the mixture for at least one hour.

2. To make the holly wreath, place a small glass bowl upside-down in the center of a round serving dish. Drop spoonfuls of the chilled mixture around the bowl and smooth it to resemble a wreath. Remove the bowl. Decorate with parsley sprigs and arrange the pimiento pieces to resemble a bow.

Variation: Football Centerpiece *Form spread into the shape of a football on an oblong platter. Use the parsley stems or thin pimiento strips to form the laces on the football. Surround the base with parsley sprigs to resemble a "grass playing field".*

Make the appetizer and place in an airtight container or "dipping dish" covered tightly with plastic wrap. Place on a serving platter, add a jar of pimientos, a bunch of parsley, **"Toasted Bagel Chips"** *(pg. 67), and decorative serving spreaders.*

Macadamia Nut Hummus

Makes 1-3/4 cups

Here's a new flavor to the basic hummus.

1/2 cup roasted, unsalted macadamia nuts
2 tablespoons extra virgin olive oil
1 to 2 garlic cloves, peeled
3 tablespoons water
12 lemon basil leaves
freshly ground black pepper, to taste
2 cups canned garbanzo beans, drained
2 tablespoons fresh lemon juice
salt, to taste

1. Place all ingredients in a food processor fitted with a metal blade. Process until ingredients are smooth. If not using immediately, cover and refrigerate.

    Use as a dip for fresh vegetables or spread on crackers or **"Pocket Bread Toast Triangles"** *(pg. 66).*

Great when someone asks for a "chip and dip" set. Place the hummus in the dip container, cover with plastic wrap, and add bundles of veggie sticks wrapped in colored plastic wrap tied with raffia.

Many Layer Dip

Serves 12 to 16

This may be made a day in advance, but tightly seal the avocado layer with the sour cream layer to prevent the avocado from darkening.

3 ripe avocados
2 tablespoons bottled lemon juice
salt, to taste
freshly ground black pepper, to taste
1 cup sour cream
1/2 cup mayonnaise
2 (9 ounce) cans bean dip
1 cup sliced green onions (tops included)
3 tomatoes, chopped
1 (3.8 ounce) can sliced black olives
1/2 pound shredded sharp Cheddar cheese
1 cup picante sauce
tortillas chips for dipping

1. Scoop avocados out of the skin and mash in a bowl. Add the lemon juice, salt and pepper; stir to blend. Set aside.

2. Combine sour cream and mayonnaise in a separate bowl. Set aside.

3. To assemble, layer ingredients in a 13 x 9-inch dish in the following order: bean dip, mashed avocados, sour cream mixture, green onions, tomatoes, olives, cheese, and picante sauce. Serve with chips.

Gift Giving

This is most attractive layered in a clear dish, but don't limit yourself. Include a basket of tortilla chips so you can dive right in!

Overnight Guacamole Taco Dip

Serve 6 to 10

I love the way the flavors "melt" together when the taco seasoning starts to dissolve from the moisture in the guacamole and sour cream. Mmmmmmmmmm!

1 recipe *"Guacamole Dip"* (recipe follows)
1/2 package taco seasoning mix
1 pint sour cream

1. Spread guacamole in an even layer in a round, flat dish (layer should be 1/2 to 3/4-inch deep). Sprinkle taco seasoning over guacamole layer. Spread sour cream over the top (about 3/8-inch thick). Make sure that the sour cream seals to the edges of the dish to keep the guacamole from turning dark.

2. Cover tightly and refrigerate overnight (or at least a few hours) to let the flavors blend. Serve with tortilla chips.

Gift Giving

A colored serving dish contrasts beautifully with the sour cream topping. Cover tightly with foil or plastic wrap and include your favorite tortilla chips for dipping. Package this in a special basket or wrap with a piece of clear cellophane.

Guacamole Dip

2 to 3 ripe avocados
3 to 4 tablespoons water
1/4 teaspoon garlic powder
1/8 teaspoon seasoned pepper
2 to 6 drops Tabasco sauce

1. Scoop the avocados out of the skins and place in medium bowl. Mash with a fork. Add water and mix well. (The water will make the avocado texture smooth.) Add garlic powder, pepper, and Tabasco. Mix well.

    Note: *When I make guacamole for dipping, I increase the seasoning.*

Sun-Dried Tomato Torte

Serves 8 to 10

Indulge yourself and impress your friends with this irresistible creation, but if you're concerned about calories, you needn't bother with this treat.

1 (8 ounce) package cream cheese, at room temperature
1/2 pound unsalted butter, at room temperature
1 cup grated Parmesan cheese
1/2 cup sun-dried tomatoes packed in oil, drained
2 tablespoons oil from the sun-dried tomatoes
2 cups lightly packed fresh basil leaves
**1 recipe *"Pocket Bread Toast Triangles" (pg. 66)*
    or crackers, for serving**

1. Process cream cheese, butter, and Parmesan cheese until smooth in a food processor fitted with a metal blade.

2. Cut 4 tomatoes into strips and set aside.

3. Add the remaining tomatoes, oil, and most of the basil leaves (reserve a few for garnishing). Process mixture until blended.

4. Cover the mixture and chill for 20 minutes or until firm enough to hold a shape. Mold the mixture into a round "cake shape" on a round serving platter. Cover and chill until ready to serve. (This may be prepared up to 3 days in advance.)

5. To serve, bring to room temperature. Garnish with the reserved tomato strips and fresh basil leaves. Accompany with the ***"Pocket Bread Toast Triangles"*** or crackers.

*The perfect gift for someone who requests a serving platter or that special collectible plate. Include a coordinating bowl or cup filled with the rich torte mixture. Add a bundle of fresh basil leaves, a jar of sun-dried tomato strips (packed in oil), a spreading knife and **"Pocket Bread Toast Triangles"** (pg. 66).*

Nine Bean Soup Mix

Makes 1 gift

This is one of my favorite gifts to give. The layered colors are spectacular when presented in a glass jar. One pound of each bean will yield ten gifts.

1/4 cup each dried:
black beans, yellow split peas, pinto or Anasazi beans,
pink lentils, black-eyed beans, green split peas, kidney
beans, white navy beans, garbanzo beans or chick-peas

Seasoning Mix:
1/4 cup dried minced onion
1/4 cup dried parsley
1 tablespoon salt
2 bay leaves
1 teaspoon garlic powder
1 teaspoon dried basil

1. Layer the beans, starting with the black beans, in the order listed in a one pint or larger glass canning jar.

2. Combine the seasoning mix and store in a separate airtight container or bag. Tie the bag on the one pint jar, or if using a larger jar, place the bag in the jar on top of the beans.

Gift Giving

The color of the beans is festive enough, but if you must, attach a bunch of dried lavender tied with raffia with the preparation instructions.

Preparation Instructions to Include with Soup Mix:

Makes 8 cups soup

- Rinse the beans. Place in a large pot with water to cover (about 3 cups). Bring to a boil. Keep at a boil for 5 minutes. Turn the heat off and cover the beans. Let stand for 1 hour.

- Drain liquid from beans. Add 8 cups of fresh water along with the contents of the seasoning packet. Bring mixture to a boil; reduce the heat to low. Cover and simmer for about 2 hours or until the beans are tender.

- Remove 1 cup of beans and mash in a separate bowl. Return the mashed beans to the pot. Simmer uncovered for about 40 minutes or until the soup has thickened.

- Garnish ideas: chopped tomatoes, chopped cilantro, shredded mozzarella cheese, a dollop of sour cream or plain yogurt.......

   Variation: *Beans may be cooked with a ham bone, salt pork, or any vegetables. Add the meat after soaking the beans. Add vegetables during the last 30 to 40 minutes.*

About Seasonings & Spices

Mixed seasonings are available in most supermarkets, but by making your own blends, your personal touch is added by adjusting the seasonings to your liking.

If you've got a green thumb and grow herbs, save some for drying. Fresh-dried herbs have a magnificent flavor. Once air-dried, crumble the leaves and use them in your own "house blends".

Here are a few of my favorite combinations. They may be doubled or tripled, but stir well to evenly distribute the ingredients.

Cajun Spice

Makes 1-3/4 cups

This can be used for seasoning chicken, beef, fish, or pork. I like to add it to a basic oil and vinegar salad dressing for a zing!

1/4 cup garlic powder
1/4 cup onion powder
2/3 cup paprika
2 tablespoons cayenne pepper
2 tablespoons freshly ground white pepper
1 tablespoon freshly ground black pepper
2 tablespoons dried oregano
2 tablespoons dried thyme

1. Combine all ingredients in a mixing bowl. Stir by hand to blend.

    Store in an airtight container.

Gift Giving

Place in a decorative crock or shaker bottle. The shaker can then be placed on the table for adding additional flavor…but I strongly suggest advising your guests of the contents before they liberally sprinkle this one on their meal!

Curry Powder

Makes about 1/4 cup

This is a unique combination of flavors usually associated with East Indian dishes. Use whenever curry powder is called for, sprinkle over steamed veggies, or add a dash to your salad in place of pepper.

1 bay leaf
2 teaspoons black peppercorns
2 teaspoons red crushed pepper
1 tablespoon ground turmeric
1-1/2 teaspoons ground cardamom
1-1/2 teaspoons whole cloves
1-1/2 teaspoons whole coriander seed
3/4 teaspoon whole cumin
3/4 teaspoon ground nutmeg
1 (3 inch) cinnamon stick, broken into pieces

1. Place all ingredients in a coffee grinder or blender fitted with a sharp blade. Grind the ingredients to a powder.

   Store in an airtight container.

Package in a decorative container with a wide mouth. Tie on a small spoon for accessing this highly aromatic blend.

Herbs of Provence

Makes about 1-1/3 cups

This versatile blend of flavors is often overlooked. Here are a few ways I use this blend.

- *rub onto meats or poultry before roasting or grilling*
- *place a couple of spoonfuls in the cavity of a whole turkey or chicken before roasting*
- *add to softened cream cheese, sour cream, or plain yogurt for a veggie dip or a baked potato topping*

1/4 cup dried marjoram
1/4 cup dried oregano
1/4 cup dried summer savory
1/4 cup dried thyme
3 tablespoons dried basil
3 teaspoons dried rosemary, crumbled
1 teaspoon dried sage, crumbled
1 teaspoon fennel seeds
1 bay leaf, crumbled

1. Combine ingredients in a bowl and stir to blend.

   Store in an airtight container.

Gift Giving

Be generous when giving this blend....a stoneware or pottery crock with a tight-fitting top is exceptionally appropriate for this "old world" blend. Tie on a small bundle of dried flowers or herbs.

Italian Herb Seasoning

Makes about 2/3 cup

Add to your favorite Italian dish or simply brush chicken pieces lightly with olive oil and rub the herbs into the surface before grilling or baking. Compliment the chicken by combining a spoonful of seasoning with softened butter to spread on French bread.

2 tablespoons dried basil
2 tablespoons dried marjoram
2 tablespoons dried oregano
2 tablespoons dried parsley
1 tablespoon fennel seeds
1 tablespoon dried rosemary
1 tablespoon dried thyme
2 bay leaves, crumbled

1. Combine all ingredients in a mixing bowl. Toss lightly to blend.

    Store in an airtight container.

Combine the seasoning with softened butter and spoon into a ramekin. Include a jar of the seasoning, a loaf of French bread, and a knife for spreading. (Keep the butter refrigerated until time to deliver the gift.)

About Pesto Paste

There is nothing better than the aroma of fresh basil, unless it's the aroma of pesto paste. I add only enough olive oil to blend the ingredients which keeps it quite thick, therefore the name "pesto paste". This permits the chef to select the ingredient of their choice for thinning....olive oil, pasta water (water leftover after cooking pasta), chicken or vegetable stock, or even white wine.

I keep at least three varieties of pesto paste tucked in my freezer for gifts or just for me! Spread it on bread, pizza rounds, crackers, toss with warm pasta (adding a little "pasta water" to thin the paste), or add a spoonful to salad dressings.

Thanks go out to my best pal, Judy, for always having at least five varieties of basil in the garden (one year we had eleven). With this selection, the possibilities for different pesto pastes are never ending.

Here are six of my favorites...

A decorative crock or any container with a wide mouth is great. Include a small serving spoon as a "tie-on".

Basic Pesto Paste

Makes 2-1/2 cups

This is as it says, basic, and a staple in the freezer.

1/4 cup toasted pine nuts
2 cups tightly packed fresh basil leaves
2 cups tightly packed spinach leaves
4 garlic cloves, peeled
1 cup grated Parmesan cheese
1/4 teaspoon salt
1/4 cup extra virgin olive oil
1/4 to 1/2 cup water

1. Place pine nuts, basil, spinach, garlic, cheese, and salt in a food processor fitted with a metal blade. Turn on motor and add the olive oil in a stream. Process until a smooth paste is formed.

2. Slowly add the water with the motor running. Process until smooth and well combined, but not runny.

   Refrigerate in an airtight container or freeze in smaller portions.

   Note: *I like to add only enough olive oil to maintain the freshness of the herbs. Add additional olive oil or "pasta water" (water left over after cooking pasta) at time of use to attain desired consistency.*

Not-So-Rich Pesto Paste

Makes 2 cups

This is for those of you who keep an eye on fat intake.

3 garlic cloves, peeled
1-1/2 cups fresh or canned chicken broth
6 cups lightly packed fresh basil leaves
3 tablespoons extra virgin olive oil
1-1/2 teaspoons Kosher or rock salt

1. Process garlic and broth in a food processor fitted with a metal blade. With the motor running, add basil, oil, and salt. Continue processing until smooth.

   Refrigerate in an airtight container or freeze in smaller portions.

   Note: *Add additional broth or "pasta water" (water left over after cooking pasta) to attain desired consistency at time of use.*

Macadamia Nut
Pesto Paste

Here's a new twist on an old basic. The flavor from the mac nuts is a bit milder and sweeter than the traditional pine nuts.

1/2 cup roasted, unsalted macadamia nuts
2 cups tightly packed fresh basil leaves
1/2 cup fresh Italian flat-leaf parsley
4 garlic cloves, peeled
freshly ground salt, to taste
1/4 cup extra virgin olive oil
1 tablespoon hot pepper oil (optional)

1. Place nuts, basil, parsley, garlic, and salt into a food processor fitted with a metal blade. Turn on and slowly add the oil until a paste forms. Scrape down the bowl and process until smooth.

   Refrigerate in an airtight container or freeze in smaller portions.

Red Basil Pesto Paste

Makes 2-1/2 cups

If you grow herbs and haven't tried opal basil, you're missing out. The unusual, unique color of the pesto paste will arouse the curiosity of your family or guests.

2 cups lightly packed fresh opal basil leaves
2-1/2 tablespoons sun-dried tomatoes, packed in oil
2 garlic cloves, peeled
1/2 cup grated Romano or Parmesan cheese
1/3 cup toasted pine nuts
1/2 cup extra virgin olive oil
salt, to taste
freshly ground black pepper, to taste

1. Place the basil, tomatoes, garlic, cheese, and pine nuts in a food processor fitted with a metal blade. While the machine is running, slowly add the olive oil and process until smooth. Season with salt and pepper.

   Refrigerate in an airtight container or freeze in smaller portions.

   Note: *Recipe may be doubled, but DO NOT double the amount of olive oil, use only 1/2 cup.*

Roasted Pepper Pesto Paste

Makes 2 cups

If you're really energetic, roast your own peppers, but you may need to add extra virgin olive oil to form the paste.

1/2 cup fresh Italian flat-leaf parsley
1-1/2 cups tightly packed fresh basil leaves
1 (11-1/2 ounce) jar roasted bell peppers (yellow, red, or
   a combination of the two), drained
4 garlic cloves, peeled
1/3 cup toasted pine nuts
salt, to taste
freshly ground black pepper, to taste

1. Place all ingredients in a food processor fitted with a metal blade. Process until ingredients form a "paste". If the mixture is too thick, add 1 teaspoon oil from the roasted red peppers. Repeat, if necessary.

Refrigerate in an airtight container or freeze in smaller portions.

Sun-Dried Tomato Pesto Paste

Makes about 1-1/2 cups

The tart, sweet flavor of the tomatoes combined with a hint of chiles and the sweetness of balsamic vinegar is unique and wonderful. Try this as a spread on sourdough bread.

1 cup sun-dried tomatoes (not packed in olive oil)
1/4 cup boiling water
5 garlic cloves, peeled
1/3 cup extra virgin olive oil
1/4 teaspoon freshly ground black pepper
1/4 teaspoon crushed pequin chiles *
1 teaspoon balsamic vinegar
1 tablespoon chopped fresh basil
3/4 teaspoon salt

* If pequin chiles are not available, substitute crushed red peppers.

1. Place the sun-dried tomatoes in a heatproof bowl or measuring cup. Pour the boiling water over the tomatoes and let stand 15 minutes. DO NOT DRAIN LIQUID FROM TOMATOES.

2. Place all ingredients (including the tomato water) in a food processor fitted with a metal blade. Process until the mixture is "chunky" yet somewhat smooth.

    Refrigerate in an airtight container or freeze in smaller portions.

About Salad Dressing

No matter how much I like a salad dressing, I'm always searching for a better one. As a result of my quest, I have included a diverse group of dressings for your sampling.

When combining foods, keep the flavor of the dressing in mind. For example: a mix of baby salad greens with diced papaya and red onion slices would nicely blend with the flavor of **"Papaya Seed Salad Dressing"** *(pg. 47).*

Don't hesitate to experiment. Try a variety of salad greens, add orange wedges, diced apples, sliced strawberries, toasted nuts, or all of the above. Now, don't stop here, keep your imagination working.

Gift Giving

Select unusual bottles or decorative cruets for the salad dressings. A bag of seasonings, such as **"Cajun Spice Mix"** *(pg. 31) or* **"Herbs of Provence"** *(pg. 33), tied to the bottle will allow your chef to use their imagination. How about a salad bowl filled with salad makings, a bottle of home-made salad dressing and bag of* **"The Best Homemade Croutons"** *(pg. 102).*

Balsamic Vinaigrette

Makes 1 cup

*Include a bag of **"Italian Herb Seasoning"** (pg. 34) with a bottle of the dressing and the dressing recipe.*

2 garlic cloves, peeled & minced
1 tablespoon Dijon-style mustard
3 tablespoons balsamic vinegar
2/3 cup extra virgin olive oil
1 tablespoon *"Italian Herb Seasoning"* (pg.34)
freshly ground black pepper, to taste
salt, to taste

1. Combine all ingredients in a jar or bottle with a tight fitting lid. Shake to combine. Refrigerate until ready to use.

Mustard Dressing

Makes 2 cups

My friends find it hard to believe that I can make a salad dressing without garlic, but here it is!

1 cup salad oil (canola, corn, or vegetable)
1/2 cup white wine vinegar
1/4 cup chopped fresh Italian flat-leaf parsley
1 tablespoon Dijon-style mustard
1 teaspoon salt
1/2 teaspoon freshly ground black pepper

1. Combine ingredients in a jar or bottle with a tight fighting lid. Shake to combine. Refrigerate until ready to use.

Chive-Mustard Dressing

Makes 1 cup

Do you ever tire of oil and vinegar based salad dressings? Give this one a try.

1 cup plain yogurt
2 teaspoons Dijon-style mustard
1 teaspoon honey
1 tablespoon fresh lemon juice
1 tablespoon finely chopped fresh chives

1. Combine all ingredients in a bowl and mix well. Cover and refrigerate for several hours to allow flavors to blend.

Fruit Vinaigrette

Makes 1-1/4 cups

Try this on steamed veggies in place of butter or cheese sauce.

1/2 cup fruit-flavored vinegar
1/2 cup canola oil
1 teaspoon soy sauce
1 teaspoon honey
1 teaspoon Dijon-style mustard
1 teaspoon fresh lime juice
2 garlic cloves, minced
2 tablespoons finely chopped fresh basil leaves

1. Whisk together all ingredients except the basil. After combined, stir in basil. Use immediately or refrigerate until ready to use.

Chinese Black Bean Vinaigrette

Makes 2 cups

Some of these ingredients may be difficult to find. If your supermarket doesn't have an Oriental food section, seek out an Asian market.

1/4 cup hoisin sauce
1/4 cup unseasoned rice vinegar
2 tablespoons granulated sugar
1/4 cup sesame oil
1/4 cup chopped green onions
1/4 cup soy sauce
1/4 cup Chinese black beans
1/2 cup canola oil
1 tablespoon toasted sesame seeds

1. Place all ingredients in a blender and process until the beans are chopped and ingredients have emulsified. Refrigerate until ready to use.

   Serve over a tossed salad of Napa cabbage, romaine pieces, sliced almonds, chopped green onions, radish slivers, and shredded carrots.

My Dressing

Makes 3 cups

What a list of ingredients! Get your taste buds ready because this is delectable.

2/3 cup extra virgin olive oil
2/3 cup salad oil (canola, corn or vegetable)
1/3 cup mayonnaise
1/3 cup red wine vinegar
1/4 cup water
4 ounces blue cheese, crumbled
2 teaspoons salt
1-1/2 teaspoons fresh lemon juice
1 teaspoon freshly ground black pepper
1 teaspoon Worcestershire sauce
1/2 teaspoon Dijon-style mustard
1/2 teaspoon granulated sugar
1 garlic clove, peeled & minced
1 egg (optional)

1. Combine all ingredients in a blender. Purée until the dressing is smooth. Refrigerate until ready to use.

   To serve, bring slightly to room temperature. Shake well and pour over your favorite salad.

Papaya Seed
Salad Dressing

This is for those of you who feel guilty when disposing of papaya seeds. Exceptionally tasty served over fresh fruit or a mixture of baby greens with pieces of "Spiced Nuts" (pg. 100).

1/2 cup granulated sugar
1/2 cup tarragon vinegar
1/2 cup white wine
1 teaspoon seasoned salt
1 teaspoon dry mustard
2 cups vegetable oil
1 small onion, minced
3 tablespoons papaya seeds

1. Combine sugar, vinegar, wine, salt, and mustard in a blender. With the blender running, gradually add the oil and onion.

2. When mixture is thoroughly blended, add papaya seeds. Process until seeds are the size of coarsely ground pepper. Refrigerate until ready to use.

Pesto Paste
Salad Dressing

Makes 1-3/4 cups

*The flavor of basil is outstanding in this simple blend. Keeping a supply of **"Pesto Paste"** (pg. 36-41) in the refrigerator or freezer comes in handy.*

3 tablespoons pesto paste
1 cup extra virgin olive oil
1/2 cup unseasoned rice wine vinegar
freshly ground black pepper, to taste

1. Combine all ingredients in a small mixing bowl. Whisk together. Chill thoroughly before using.

    Serve atop a salad of squash, pear tomatoes, and lemon cucumbers, brush over warm grilled veggies, or just toss with fresh chilled salad greens and sliced ripe tomatoes.

Vinaigrette Dressing

Makes 3-1/2 cups

There's nothing better or more versatile than a basic vinaigrette.

2 tablespoons Dijon-style mustard
1 cup red wine vinegar
2 garlic cloves, peeled
1 green onion or 1/8 medium onion
salt, to taste
freshly ground black pepper, to taste
2-1/2 cups extra virgin olive oil or canola oil

1. Combine mustard, vinegar, garlic, onion, salt and pepper in a blender or food processor fitted with a metal blade. While the machine is running, add the oil in a stream. Process to form an emulsion. Refrigerate until ready to use.

Coffee Liqueur Honey Butter

Makes 1/3 cup

This is exceptionally great on plain biscuits or croissants.

4 tablespoons unsalted butter, at room temperature
1/4 cup coffee-flavored liqueur
3 tablespoons honey

1. Combine all ingredients in a small bowl. Beat until well blended.

   Serve in small individual cups or refrigerate until ready to use.

Mound the flavored butter into a crock or ramekin. Include small knives for spreading, a basket of your favorite biscuits or croissants, and a bottle of **"Karen's Coffee Liqueur"** *(pg. 15).*

About Raw Salsas

These are not your everyday salsas. They are wonderful at any time, with chips for dipping or as a topping. To capture the flavors at their peak, use the salsa within a few days of preparation.

If your gift won't be used within a few days, consider giving the recipe, the ingredients , and a container for serving the salsa. Arrange in a flat basket or on a tray with a bag of tortilla strips. Wrap with clear cellophane and a bow.

Cilantro Salsa

Makes 1 cup

Ah...the unique flavor of cilantro. Nothing more needs to be said.

1 bundle cilantro, finely chopped
1/4 cup finely chopped onion
2 jalapeño chiles (seeds removed), finely chopped
2 garlic cloves, finely chopped
2 tablespoons red or white wine vinegar
3 tablespoons extra virgin olive oil

1. Combine all ingredients in a mixing bowl or bottle. Stir or shake to combine.

- *For a marinade, pour over item and refrigerate: overnight for chicken or pork, just a few hours for fish.*

- *For a dipping or topping salsa: chill thoroughly before serving to allow flavors to blend.*

This looks great in a clear bottle or jar with the bright cilantro color shining through. Double the recipe and keep a jar for yourself.

Mango Salsa

Makes 1 cup

Mangoes have been referred to as the "fruit of the gods" and I certainly agree. There is nothing like the flavor of a juicy, fresh mango. Would you believe this is a great topping on chocolate ice cream? Try it!

1 mango (ripe, yet firm), diced
2 tablespoons fresh lemon juice
1 tablespoon fresh lime juice
2 teaspoons minced green onion
1 jalapeño chile (seeds removed), finely chopped
1 tablespoon chopped fresh cilantro
1/4 teaspoon salt
1/4 teaspoon crushed red pepper

1. Place all ingredients in a bowl and gently stir together. Use immediately.

   Note: *If making ahead of time, mix all ingredients except the green onion and cilantro. Refrigerate up to one day. Add green onion and cilantro before serving.*

   Variations: *Add 1/4 cup diced watermelon, cantaloupe, honeydew melon, or red onion. Add one or all...your quantity will be increased by the amount you add.*

Present this colorful mixture in a covered container of cut or clear glass. This is absolutely superb served over grilled chicken or fish.

Papaya Salsa

This is wonderful on grilled chicken or fish. Don't forget to add a spoonful or two of the juice.

2 cups diced firm papayas (2 to 3)
1/2 cup chopped red bell pepper
1 jalapeño chile (seeds removed), minced
1/4 cup diced red onion
1/2 teaspoon crushed red pepper
juice from 1 lime
2 tablespoons chopped fresh cilantro

1. Gently mix papaya, red bell pepper, jalapeño, and onion. Add crushed red pepper, lime juice, and cilantro and stir.

    This will keep for one day when refrigerated.

    Note: *Make a recipe of* **"Papaya Seed Salad Dressing"** *(pg. 47) from the unused papaya seeds.*

This must be displayed in a clear container....a jar with a wide mouth is best suited for this. Include a bottle of **"Papaya Seed Salad Dressing"** *(pg. 47) with a chile pepper tied on the bottle.*

Aloha Marinade

Makes 1-1/2 cups

The unique flavor of this marinade depends on fresh ginger. Do not attempt any substitutions.

2/3 cup soy sauce
1/2 cup fruit-flavored vinegar
3 garlic cloves, minced
1 small onion, chopped
3 tablespoons chopped fresh cilantro
2 tablespoons canola or sesame oil
1 tablespoon grated fresh ginger
1/4 teaspoon cayenne pepper

1. Combine all ingredients in a bowl or jar. Mix well. If not using immediately, refrigerate. Allow to come to room temperature before using.

    Pour over food to be marinated and let sit for several hours. This is best suited for chicken or pork.

An unusual jug or bottle will give this marinade an exotic look. If you've used mango or papaya flavored vinegar, include a jar of ***"Mango Salsa"*** *(pg. 53) or* ***"Papaya Salsa"*** *(pg. 54).*

Flank Steak Marinade   *Makes about 1-3/4 cups*

*This recipe is from my husband's childhood. It is also his standard "birthday dinner" request accompanied by **"Simply, Rice Dish"** (pg. 108). Do not skimp on the marinating time, as the flavor will be weak. Plan ahead on this one.*

> **3/4 cup canola or vegetable oil**
> **1/2 cup soy sauce**
> **3 tablespoons honey**
> **2 tablespoons red wine vinegar**
> **2 tablespoons garlic salt**
> **1 bundle green onion tops, sliced**

1. Combine the above ingredients in a bowl or jar. Stir or shake to blend. Use immediately or refrigerate until ready to use (let mixture come to room temperature before using).

   To marinate: Place flank steak flat in a shallow dish. Refrigerate for <u>no less than 24 hours</u>. Turn often for even marinade absorption.

   Barbecue or broil for <u>5 minutes a side</u>; do not overcook! To serve, slice on bias.

Present in a jar or bottle. Attach a set of barbecue tongs and a barbecue brush. Include a note about using the marinade.

Spicy Soy Sauce

Makes 1/2 gallon

This Hawaii-found recipe makes ordinary soy sauce a thing of the past. Prepare this at least three months in advance of the time you want to use it.

6 cups soy sauce
1-1/2 cups apple cider or rice vinegar
1 to 1-1/2 cups whole dried red chiles (2 to 3 inches in length)

1. Place all ingredients in a 1/2 gallon bottle with a wide neck and a plastic lid. Shake well and store in a dark place for at least 3 months (6 months is better).

2. Every once in a while, shake the bottle to blend the ingredients. The chiles will eventually soak up the liquid and start to sink.

   Note: *This recipe may be doubled or even tripled. Use more chiles if you want more of a "kick".*

Gift Giving

I love to recycle wine bottles for this sauce, but you have to add the chiles by hand. When packaging in smaller containers for gift-giving don't forget to include the soggy chiles. They may be chopped and used as a topping. (I like to put a little bowl on the table for our friends with cast-iron taste buds.)

"For-A-Group" Chocolate Eclair

Makes 24 (2-1/4 inch) squares

Kids love to help with this one. Make sure the mixing bowl lid fits tightly!

1 pound whole graham crackers
1 (6 serving size) package instant pudding and pie filling
  (vanilla, french vanilla, or banana)
3 cups milk
1 (13 ounce) container frozen whipped topping,
  slightly thawed
1 (16 ounce) can prepared chocolate frosting

1. Divide graham crackers into thirds. Layer 1/3 of the graham crackers in 13 x 9-inch rectangular dish. Set aside.

2. Combine pudding mix and milk in a large mixing bowl with a tight fighting lid. Shake container to mix. Add whipped topping and continue shaking until well combined.

3. Layer 1/2 of pudding mixture over graham crackers, repeat with a second layer of graham crackers, second half of pudding, and remaining graham crackers.

4. Spread frosting over the final layer of graham crackers. (If frosting is too thick to spread easily, remove the lid and foil seal and place container in microwave on high for 30 seconds; stir and check consistency. Repeat if necessary, but do not overheat!)

5. Cover and refrigerate at least 3 hours. Cut into squares and serve, making sure all layers are presented in each serving.

Gift Giving

This is for those of you who have a hard time giving empty storage containers as gifts. In addition to a large rectangular container, include a set of bowls with lids and the packaged ingredients.

Some Cooking

They're still easy, but do require one step of cooking. If they weren't worth the effort, they wouldn't be here!

Dips & Doodles
Cheese & Olive Tidbits
Corned Beef Nibbles
Hot Layered Bean Dip
Yummy Dip
Pocket Bread Toast Triangles
Toasted Bagel Chips
Coffee Liqueur Fruit Dip

On Top & Around:
Coffee Liqueur Barbecue Sauce
Horseradish Cream
"Some Cooking" Salsas
- Almost Rosie's Salsa
- Green Salsa
- Tomatillo Salsa
Curry-Tarragon Dressing

In the Middle:
Yams, Yams, & More Yams
- Apricot Baked Yams
- Easy Baked Yams
- Maple Candy Yams
Baked Fruit Delight
Pickled Peaches
Sweet Pickle Chips

When All Is Said & Done:
Spiced Lemon Pears
Stuffed Baked Apples
White Compote
Chocolate Dipped Pretzels
English Toffee
Real Good Dessert
Karen's Macadamia Nut Fudge
Whole Grain Jam Squares

Cheese & Olive Tidbits

Makes 1 cup (serves 12 to 16)

These tasty, open-faced goodies are great accompaniments to a "soup and salad" meal.

1 (4-1/4 ounce) can chopped olives
2/3 pound sharp Cheddar cheese, shredded
1/2 cup tomato sauce
Tabasco sauce, to taste
garlic salt, to taste
2 tablespoons finely chopped onion (red or white)
1 loaf hors d'oeuvre or cocktail size bread

1. Combine olives, cheese, tomato sauce, Tabasco, garlic salt, and onion in a mixing bowl. Cover and chill to allow flavors to blend.

   To serve, spread mixture on bread slices. Broil until cheese melts. Serve immediately. Leftover spread may be stored in the refrigerator.

Gift Giving

Purchase two sizes of plastic storage containers, one larger than the other, but select sizes that look proportionate to each other when stacked. Place the prepared olive and cheese mixture in the small container, the bread in the large one. Stack the containers, tie with ribbon or raffia and attach a wooden cooking utensil.

Corned Beef Nibbles

Makes 1-3/4 cups (serves 20 to 24)

For a meal, cut whole pieces of pocket bread rounds in half, stuff with the corned beef mixture and shredded cabbage or lettuce.

1/3 cup mayonnaise
2-1/2 tablespoons yellow or Dijon-style mustard
1 teaspoon vinegar (any flavor)
1 teaspoon granulated sugar
1/2 teaspoon prepared horseradish
1/4 teaspoon paprika
1 (12 ounce) can corned beef, chilled
1/2 pound Swiss cheese, shredded
8 green onions, sliced
1 recipe *"Pocket Bread Toast Triangles"* (pg. 66)

1. Combine mayonnaise, mustard, vinegar, sugar, horseradish, and paprika in a small bowl. Set aside.

2. In a medium bowl, break-up the corned beef with a fork. Add cheese and green onions. Mix well. Add mayonnaise mixture; stir until combined.

3. Spread on ***"Pocket Bread Toast Triangles"*** and serve. Prepare just before serving as toast may get soggy. Refrigerate unused mixture.

Gift Giving

*A great way to dress up a "utility" gift. Spoon mixture into a glass measuring cup. Sit the measuring cup in the middle of a mixing bowl and place **"Pocket Bread Toast Triangles"** (pg. 66) around the measuring cup. Cover tightly and attach a set of measuring spoons.*

Hot Layered Bean Dip

Serves 8 to 10

A great dip for any kind of weather. Not only is this easy to prepare, but assemble it the night before and bake before serving.

1 (8 ounce) package cream cheese, at room temperature
1 (9 ounce) can bean dip
20 drops Tabasco sauce (adjust to your taste)
1 cup sour cream
1/2 cup sliced green onions
1 (1 ounce) package taco seasoning mix
3/4 cup shredded Monterey Jack cheese
3/4 cup shredded Cheddar cheese
tortilla chips for dipping

1. Preheat oven to 350°F. Spray an ovenproof, shallow baking dish with no-stick cooking spray.

2. Combine cream cheese, bean dip, Tabasco, sour cream, onions, and seasoning in a mixing bowl. Spread into the prepared dish. Top with a layer of each cheese. (If making the day ahead, cover and refrigerate. Allow to come to room temperature before baking.)

3. Bake 20 to 25 minutes or until cheese has melted and is bubbly around the edges. Serve warm with tortilla chips.

    Variation: *Plain yogurt may be substituted for sour cream. Reduced fat (not fat-free) cheese may be substituted.*

Prepare the dip in the shallow dish, but do not bake. Cover the top with plastic wrap or foil and include baking instructions. Wrap with clear cellophane and finish with a bow.

Yummy Dip

Makes 3 cups (serves 12 to 14)

This can only be described as "just plain good". Another dish to assemble up to a day in advance.

1 (14 ounce) can artichoke hearts in water, drained
1 cup grated Parmesan cheese
1 cup mayonnaise
1 (7 ounce) can diced green chiles
1 tablespoon garlic powder
"Toasted Bagel Chips" (pg. 67) or crackers

1. Preheat oven to 325°F. Spray an ovenproof, shallow baking dish with no-stick cooking spray.

2. Place artichokes, cheese, mayonnaise, chiles, and garlic powder into a food processor fitted with a metal blade. Process until well combined and somewhat "chunky".

3. Transfer mixture to prepared baking dish. (At this point, the dip may be tightly covered and refrigerated. Allow to come to room temperature before baking.) Bake for 30 minutes or until edges are bubbly. Serve warm with a basket of ***Toasted Bagel Chips*** or crackers.

Gift Giving

*Bake in a round shallow quiche dish. Place in a basket larger than the quiche dish and fill with **"Toasted Bagel Chips"** (pg. 67). If dip won't be consumed immediately, assemble and cover with aluminum foil. Include baking instructions.*

Pocket Bread
Toast Triangles

Makes 72 triangles

These are great to have on hand, so don't hesitate to make up extras. For variation in flavor and color, mix together different varieties of pita bread.

6 rounds of Pita Pocket Bread

1. Preheat oven to 400°F. Split rounds in half lengthwise so you have two full rounds out of each bread. Cut each round into six triangles. Place on baking sheets in a single layer.

2. Bake for 5 minutes or until lightly toasted. Let cool completely before using. Store leftovers in an airtight container.

These are a great accompaniment to any gift of dip or cheese. Package in different colored cellophane bags for an assortment of bundles.

Toasted Bagel Chips

Makes any amount you desire

This is a great way to use any "leftover" or semi-stale bagels. Of course, fresh ones work well, too!

whole bagels, any size, any flavor, any quantity

1. Preheat oven to 400°F. Slice bagels lengthwise in 1/4-inch thick slices. (A device made to hold bagels for cutting is strongly recommended.)

2. Place the slices on a baking sheet in a single layer. Bake for 3 to 5 minutes; turn slices over. Bake 3 to 5 minutes longer or until pieces are golden. (Baking time may vary with thickness and freshness of bagels.)

3. Let bagel slices cool completely on baking sheet before breaking them in half. Store in an airtight container.

Package these in different shapes of colored tins as accompaniments to dips and spreads.

Coffee Liqueur Fruit Dip

Makes 2-1/2 cups

A light and refreshing dip for a brunch or dessert. Let your imagination work overtime when selecting a variety of fresh seasonal fruits.

1/4 cup honey
1/4 cup orange juice
1/2 cup plus 1 tablespoon *"Karen's Coffee Liqueur"*
  (pg. 15)
1 cup frozen whipped topping, thawed

1. Combine honey, orange juice and liqueur in a medium saucepan. Cook over low heat, stirring constantly, until the mixture coats the back of a spoon. Remove from heat and let cool.

2. When mixture has cooled completely, fold in whipped topping.

   Serve with a variety of fresh or dried fruits.

Using a "chip and dip" bowl, place the dip in the serving bowl. Select large pieces of seasonal fruit and cut into quarters; wrap each one with plastic wrap. Include whole pieces of smaller fruits. If traveling with this gift, you may wish to substitute a variety of dried fruit pieces for dipping.

Coffee Liqueur Barbecue Sauce

Makes 1-1/2 cups

This is not your everyday barbecue sauce. The special ingredients make it one of the most luscious sauces I've ever tasted.

3/4 cup *"Karen's Coffee Liqueur"* (pg. 15)
1/2 cup prepared chili sauce
3 tablespoons canned pineapple juice
1/4 cup cold water
2 tablespoons cornstarch

1. Combine liqueur, chili sauce, and pineapple juice in a small saucepan over medium-low heat.

2. In a small bowl, add cornstarch to water; stir until dissolved. Slowly add cornstarch mixture to liqueur mixture, stirring constantly. Heat until sauce starts to thicken and the cornstarch "cloudiness" is clear.

Refrigerate up to 2 weeks.

Note: *This is enough sauce for 3 pounds of ribs or chicken. For barbecuing: baste meats during the last 20 minutes of cooking, turning and basting often. May also be baked in a 350°F oven, basting often.*

Gift Giving

Package in a bottle with a basting brush and a set of barbecue tongs. A few chiles tied on with raffia will complete the gift.

Horseradish Cream

Makes 1-1/2 cups

Serve this accompaniment whenever you would serve horseradish.

2 tablespoons unsalted butter, at room temperature
2 tablespoons all-purpose flour
1 cup stock (beef, chicken, or vegetable)
2 tablespoons prepared horseradish
1-1/2 tablespoons Dijon-style mustard
1/2 cup sour cream
1/2 cup whipping cream
1 tablespoon fresh lemon juice

1. Melt butter in a medium saucepan over medium heat. Whisk in flour. Cook for 2 minutes, stirring constantly.

2. Whisk in stock. Add horseradish and mustard. Cook an additional 2 minutes. Remove from heat and stir in sour cream.

3. After ingredients are well combined, add whipping cream and lemon juice. Heat over low just until warm...DO NOT BOIL! Use immediately or refrigerate until ready to use.

    For a richer flavor, substitute the cooking liquid from boiled meat, such as corned beef, for the stock.

Use a decorative jar and attach a small spoon for serving right out of the jar. If your gift receiver collects spoons, this may be a great time to add one to their collection from a special place you have visited.

"Some Cooking" Salsas

Unknown to most of us, some salsas require some amount of cooking to achieve the unique flavors we enjoy.

Patience is the key element when making the following salsas, as they need to be thoroughly chilled before serving.

Gift Giving

Use any container that will let the beauty of the colors show-off. My favorite is a canning jar. Be generous with the portions and include a bag of your favorite tortilla chips for immediate tasting. For a "chile pepper" theme, include chile pepper candles, dishes decorated with chile peppers, and a serving spoon with a chile pepper for a handle!

Almost Rosie's Salsa

For those of you who know my friend, Rosie, you know how well she guards her recipe for this magnificent salsa.....this is as close as anyone will get to the real thing!

5 to 6 fresh yellow chiles
2 bundles green onions
1 bundle fresh cilantro
1 (28 ounce) can whole peeled tomatoes, undrained
1 tablespoon crushed or minced "jarred" garlic
1 tablespoon salt

1. Place chiles in a saucepan of boiling water. Boil, uncovered, for 10 minutes. Remove chiles from water and drain on paper towels. Pull off the stems.

2. While chiles are cooking, rinse green onions and cilantro. Cut-off root ends. Discard any wilted or brown pieces.

3. Slice green onions (tops included) 1/8 to 1/4-inch thick. Roughly chop cilantro. Place onions and cilantro in a large mixing bowl. Set aside.

4. Place tomatoes (juice included) into food processor fitted with a metal blade. Add cooked chiles, garlic, and salt. Process to a liquid. Pour tomato mixture into onions and cilantro. Stir by hand until blended. Cover and refrigerate. Serve after salsa is thoroughly chilled.

   Note: *"Jarred" garlic can be found in the produce department of your supermarket.*

Green Salsa

Makes 3 cups

In my opinion, there is nothing more divine than salsa made with tomatillos. This unique fruit has a one of a kind flavor.

2 tablespoons unsalted butter
1 onion, sliced
12 tomatillos (husks removed), cut into quarters
2 garlic cloves, peeled
1 bundle fresh cilantro, stems removed
3 cups water
salt, to taste

1. Melt butter in a skillet. Add onions and sauté until translucent.

2. Place sautéed onions, tomatillos, garlic, cilantro, and water in a blender or food processor fitted with a metal blade; purée.

3. Place mixture into the onion skillet and bring to a boil. Turn heat to low and simmer 5 minutes. Add salt, if desired. Chill before using.

Tomatillo Salsa

Makes 1 cup

This one is "not so mild". Adjust the heat by adding more or less of the jalapeño chile.

1 tablespoon unsalted butter
3 garlic cloves, peeled & minced
1/2 pound tomatillos (husks removed), diced
1 jalapeño chile (seeds removed), diced
1/2 red bell pepper, finely diced
3 tablespoons fresh lime juice
1/4 teaspoon freshly ground black pepper
3 tablespoons chopped fresh cilantro
1/2 teaspoon salt

1. Melt butter in a skillet. Add garlic and sauté until golden. Add tomatillos, jalapeño, bell pepper, lime juice, and black pepper. Stir to combine.

2. Remove skillet from heat. Stir in cilantro and salt. May be served at room temperature or chilled.

Curry-Tarragon Dressing

Makes 3/4 cup

This unique dressing works well over pasta or steamed veggies. Try a chilled salad of cooked rotini pasta, leftover chicken breasts, steamed broccoli, and chopped red bell pepper.

1 tablespoon canola oil
1-1/2 teaspoons curry powder
2/3 cup mayonnaise
1-1/4 teaspoons salt
1 teaspoon dried tarragon leaves, crushed
1/4 teaspoon freshly ground black pepper

1. Heat oil in a skillet over medium heat. When oil is hot, add curry powder; cook, stirring constantly, about 30 seconds. Transfer to a mixing bowl.

2. Add mayonnaise, salt, tarragon, and pepper to curry mixture. Stir until well combined. Refrigerate.

Gift Giving

*As an accompaniment to a bottle of this delicious dressing, include a container of **"Curry Powder"** (pg. 32) and the dressing recipe.*

Yams, Yams, & More Yams

How many times has someone requested a casserole dish "that is basic and will go with everything"? The brightly colored flesh of the yam can brighten up even the plainest white or glass casserole dish.

If you're confused by the terms "yams" and "sweet potatoes", don't fret. The veggies are similar in size and shape, but yams contain more natural sugar than sweet potatoes. They have been interchanged for years, and since they both taste great, let's just get cooking.

Gift Giving

Place ingredients in the casserole dish, include the recipe, a wooden spoon, and wrap with cellophane and a bow.

Apricot Baked Yams

Serves 6 to 8

A great one from Mom. If you choose to use fresh yams, they will need to be cooked and peeled prior to assembling the dish.

1 (29 ounce) can small whole or cut yams, drained
1/2 cup pecans, finely chopped
1/4 cup butter, salted or unsalted
3/4 cup firmly packed brown sugar
1/2 cup apricot nectar

1. Preheat oven to 350°F. Spray an 11 x 7-inch baking dish with no-stick cooking spray. Arrange yams in single layer. Press pecans into yams.

2. Melt butter in a 2-quart saucepan over medium heat. Add sugar and nectar. Cook until syrupy, about 5 minutes, stirring to make sure all of the sugar has dissolved. Slowly pour syrup over yams.

3. Bake for 30 minutes or until yams are well-glazed.

Easy Baked Yams

Serves 6 to 8

The tantalizing flavor in this dish is from a little used spice, cardamom. Thanks, Diana!

6 medium yams, dark or purple skins, grated
1 cup milk
1 teaspoon nutmeg
1 teaspoon allspice
1/2 teaspoon cardamom
2 eggs
1 cup firmly packed brown sugar
1/4 to 3/4 cup whole pecans
8 tablespoons unsalted butter, melted
6 to 8 ounces miniature marshmallows

1. Preheat oven to 400°F. Spray a round baking dish with no-stick cooking spray. Place grated yams in large mixing bowl. Set aside.

2. Combine milk, nutmeg, allspice, cardamom, eggs, and brown sugar in a medium mixing bowl. Add to yams and mix well. Spread into prepared baking dish.

3. Press pecans into yams. Pour the melted butter evenly over yams. Bake for 50 to 60 minutes or until yams are tender (a knife inserted into the center should come out clean).

4. Before serving, top with marshmallows and place under broiler until marshmallows are bubbly and lightly golden.

Maple Candy Yams

Patience while cooking will pay off once you savor the sweet, tender, gooey, glazed morsels.

2 (29 ounce) cans yams, drained
1/2 cup firmly packed brown sugar
1/2 cup real maple syrup
2 tablespoons butter, salted or unsalted
1/3 teaspoon cinnamon

1. Preheat oven to 325°F. Spray a 13 x 9-inch baking dish with no-stick cooking spray. Place yams as flat as possible in prepared dish.

2. Combine sugar, syrup, butter and cinnamon in a medium saucepan; heat until sugar is dissolved. Pour over yams.

3. Bake at least one hour, turning yams as they cook to allow the syrup to be absorbed while glazing all sides.

Baked Fruit Delight

Serves 12

Assemble this dish the night before and pop it into the oven for your morning brunch.

1 (20 ounce) can pineapple chunks, drained
1 (29 ounce) can peach halves, drained
1 (29 ounce) can pear halves, drained
1 (30 ounce) can apricot halves, drained
1 (21 ounce) can cherry pie filling

1. Place drained fruit pieces into colander. Cut larger pieces of fruit into "chunks". ("Chunks" are larger than bite-sized pieces.) Let fruit drain overnight or at least 6 hours.

2. Preheat oven to 325°F. Place fruit pieces in a 13 x 9-inch rectangular ovenproof dish. (At this point, fruit may be covered and refrigerated until morning.)

3. Top with pie filling. Bake for 25 to 30 minutes, or until fruit is hot and bubbly around the edges.

   Note: *Recipe may be cut in half by using an 8 ounce can of pineapple chunks and 15-1/4 ounce cans of peaches, pears, and apricots. I suggest using the whole can of pie filling.*

Assemble ingredients in a white casserole dish (shows off the cherry topping) and cover with pink plastic wrap. Deliver the gift ready-to-bake topped with a serving spoon and baking instructions. Look for a casserole dish that has a basket or metal carrier for that special touch.

*Mrs. Ward's Tropical
Oatmeal Delights*

Nine Bean Soup Mix

Almost Rosie's Salsa, Green Salsa,
Cilantro Salsa & Mango Salsa

Six Week
Bran Muffins

Lemon Squares

*Whole Grain
Jam Squares*

Karen's
Coffee Liqueur
& Coffee Liqueur
Fruit Dip

Cajun Spice,
Curry Powder,
Herbs of Provence
& Italian Herb
Seasoning

*Fruit Vinaigrette, Pesto Paste Salad Dressing,
Balsamic Vinaigrette, Chive-Mustard Dressing
& The Best Homemade Croutons*

Easy Baked Yams

Sun-Dried Tomato Torte &
Pocket Bread Toast Triangles

Cheese & Olive Tidbits &
Toasted Bagel Chips

Macadamia
Nut Hummus

*Chocolate
Espresso Mix*

Chris Ward's Transfusions

English Toffee & Spiced Whole Almonds

Pickled Peaches

No matter where we celebrate Thanksgiving and Christmas, my husband has to have his "Pickled Peaches". He can't remember one of these holidays without them and they compliment any main dish.

> **2 (29 ounce) cans peach halves**
> **1 cup peach syrup (reserved from canned peaches)**
> **1/2 cup granulated sugar**
> **1/2 cup apple cider vinegar**
> **1 whole (3 inch) cinnamon stick**
> **about 1/3 ounce whole cloves (4 for each peach half)**
> **1 tablespoon brandy (optional)**

1. Drain peaches, reserving 1 cup of syrup. Combine syrup, sugar, vinegar, and cinnamon stick in a 6-quart or larger cooking pot. Bring to a boil, stirring occasionally, to help sugar dissolve.

2. While liquid is heating, insert four cloves into curved side of peach halves. Push cloves in firmly so they won't easily slip out while simmering.

3. Carefully drop peach halves into the boiling liquid. Decrease heat to low and simmer for 4 minutes. Add brandy and remove the cinnamon stick. Slightly cool peaches before transferring them to an airtight container. Store in refrigerator until ready to serve.

Gift Giving

There's nothing more attractive than the color of the fruit showing through a large clear canning jar. Second choice would be a uniquely shaped glass jar. Decorate with raffia and some cinnamon sticks.

Sweet Pickle Chips

Makes about 2 quarts

Sweet pickles have never tasted so good! Once you've savored these jewels, you'll never go back to "store-bought" again!

1 cup apple cider vinegar
5 cups granulated sugar
1 (3 inch) cinnamon stick
1 tablespoon whole cloves
1 garlic clove, peeled
2 quarts whole Kosher dill pickles

1. Combine vinegar, sugar, cinnamon stick, cloves, and garlic in a 4-quart or larger saucepan. Bring mixture to a boil over medium heat, stirring frequently to dissolve sugar.

2. While liquid is heating, drain pickles. Slice pickles uniformly, about 1/4 to 3/8-inch thick. Uniformity is important for the pickles to absorb the flavors evenly. Set aside.

3. When liquid boils and sugar has dissolved, carefully add pickle slices. Simmer, uncovered, for 3 to 5 minutes. Remove pan from heat. Stir frequently until mixture has cooled. Place pickles into clean jars or airtight containers. Cover with liquid and refrigerate.

Gift Giving

Anything goes when packaging these for giving, a glass container with a tight-fitting lid or a plastic storage container. If using a canning jar, pack it in a wire basket or clay pot. You may want to include a packet of herb or flower seeds.

Spiced Lemon Pears

Serves 4 whole or 8 halves

Serve warm or chilled as a side dish or as a dessert topped with ice cream and fresh berries. This is visually tempting and easy on the taste buds.

1-1/2 cups water
1 cup firmly packed light brown sugar
1/4 cup bottled lemon juice
2 (3 inch) cinnamon sticks
6 whole cloves
4 whole pears

1. Combine water, sugar, lemon juice, cinnamon sticks, and cloves in a medium saucepan; bring to a boil. Stir occasionally to dissolve the sugar.

2. While liquid is heating, cut pears in half, peel, and remove cores and stems. When sugar is dissolved and liquid is boiling, add pears. Turn heat to low, cover and simmer 10 minutes or until pears are tender.

Gift Giving

Package the pears in a jar nestled in a basket or gift bag with a box of fresh berries, serving bowls, and spoons.

Stuffed
Baked Apples

Serves 6

I can already taste this old-fashioned treat served steaming hot with heavy cream and the sweet juice from the cooked apples. Would adding a dollop of whipped cream be too decadent?

7 tablespoons unsalted butter
1/2 cup packed raisins
boiling water (about 1 cup)
3 slices white bread
1/2 cup walnut pieces
2/3 cup granulated sugar
1 teaspoon ground cinnamon
1/8 teaspoon ground nutmeg
2 tablespoons brandy (such as Calvados)
6 large baking apples (such as Rome Beauty or
   Winesap), cored

1. Place oven rack on lowest adjustment. Preheat oven to 325°F. Using 1 tablespoon of butter, grease a baking dish large enough to hold the apples. Set aside.

2. Place raisins in a heatproof bowl and add boiling water. Set aside to allow raisins to plump (about 10 minutes). Drain raisins, reserve the water to cook the apples in.

3. Prepare apple filling in a food processor fitted with a metal blade. Process bread slices to bread crumbs. Add walnuts, sugar, cinnamon, and nutmeg. Process in one second intervals. Transfer to mixing bowl. Add drained raisins and brandy; mix well.

4. Stuff cored apples as follows: 1/2 tablespoon butter, stuffing (packed tightly), finish with another 1/2 tablespoon of butter. Repeat for all apples. Add reserved raisin water to the apple dish and cover tightly with foil.

5. Bake for 20 minutes. Remove foil and baste apples with cooking liquid. Continue baking, uncovered, for 50 to 55 minutes, basting every 15 minutes. Serve warm or at room temperature.

Place the cooked apples in crockery or earthenware dishes. You could fit three or four apples in a pie plate or baking dish. If you select individual serving dishes, place an apple in each and cover tightly. Place dishes on a serving tray for gift presentation.

White Compote

Serves 6 whole or 12 halves

Be patient with this one...slow cooking is the key.

6 pears, halved & cored
1 cup granulated sugar
1-1/2 cups water
1/2 cup anise-flavored liqueur (such as Galliano)

1. Place all ingredients in a large saucepan. Bring to a simmer, stirring occasionally to dissolve sugar. Cover and gently simmer for 10 to 15 minutes until fruit is soft.

   Pears may be served warm or chilled. Intriguing presentations range from cooking syrup spooned over the top to adding a scoop of vanilla ice cream, chocolate or raspberry sauce, and whipped cream.

   Variation: *After cooking, pears can be cut into "chunky" pieces and used as a topping for ice cream or plain cheesecake.*

Package in a wide-mouth jar, covering the fruit with the cooking syrup. A purchased cheesecake and pie server would be a great accompaniment.

Chocolate Dipped Pretzels

Makes 3 cups

These are simple and surprisingly tasty! The chocolate and salt flavors are scrumptious.

12 ounces semisweet chocolate chips
2 tablespoons shortening
1 (8 ounce) bag mini twist pretzels

1. Place a piece of parchment or waxed paper on a baking sheet. Melt half of the chips and half of the shortening in a microwavable bowl on high, using 1 minute intervals and stirring in between each minute. (Do not overheat as chocolate will harden and not re-melt.)

2. Place a pretzel into the melted chocolate, turn with a fork until coated. Remove and place on prepared baking sheet. Repeat until all pretzels and chocolate are used.

3. Refrigerate the dipped pretzels for 1 hour to set the chocolate. Store in an airtight container.

*Package in a cellophane bag and tuck them into a coffee mug. Add a second cup and include a bag of **"Chocolate Espresso Mix"** (pg. 12) and cinnamon sticks.*

English Toffee

This recipe was taught in my Junior High School Cooking Class. For an easy twist to an old favorite, substitute macadamia nut pieces for the almonds.

2 tablespoons unsalted butter for baking sheet
1 cup sliced almonds
1/2 pound unsalted butter
1 cup granulated sugar
6 (1.55 ounce) bars chocolate candy

1. Generously grease a baking sheet with turned-up sides with two tablespoons of butter. Scatter almond pieces on prepared baking sheet. Set aside.

2. In a medium saucepan, over medium-high heat, bring 1/2 pound of butter and sugar to a boil. When mixture boils, cook for 10 minutes, stirring constantly. Immediately pour the mixture over the almond slices.

3. Break chocolate bars on top of hot mixture. Allow chocolate to soften and spread with a knife. Cool completely before breaking into pieces. Store in an airtight container.

Gift Giving

*Package in a colored tin with a tight-fitting lid. Line the inside with waxed tissue paper and finish with a colorful gingham bow. Attach a bag of **"Spiced Whole Almonds"** (pg. 101).*

Real Good Dessert

Serves 6 to 8

This is an "oldie, but goodie" my mom used to make. It has been updated for the microwave to allow faster preparation and easier clean-up. No excuses though, this one MUST be made the night before!

1 (8 ounce) purchased angel food cake
2 eggs, yolks and whites separated
1 cup heavy cream
6 ounces semisweet chocolate chips
1/4 cup chopped walnuts
2/3 cup raisins

1. Break cake into bite-sized pieces (about 3 to 4 cups). Place in serving bowl.

2. In a medium bowl, beat egg whites with an electric mixer until stiff peaks form. Using the same beaters and a separate bowl, beat cream until stiff peaks form. Set both bowls aside.

3. Melt chocolate chips in a 4-quart microwavable bowl or measuring cup. Microwave on high in 1 minute intervals, stirring after each minute, until chocolate is melted. (Do not overheat, as chocolate will harden and not re-melt.)

4. Lightly beat egg yolks. Stir beaten yolks into warm chocolate. Fold in whipped cream, add beaten egg whites, nuts, & raisins. Fold until just blended. Pour over cake pieces. Refrigerate overnight.

Gift Giving

Prepare dessert in a large serving bowl. Insert candy canes or candy sticks into the cake and wrap with cellophane. (The candy sticks keep the cellophane from sticking to the dessert.) Include a large serving spoon and enjoy!

Karen's Macadamia Nut Fudge

Makes 4-1/2 pounds

This is the easiest "no fail" fudge I've ever made. If you can stir, you can create this fabulous taste sensation...and lots of it!!

2 tablespoons butter for baking dish
3 (8 ounce) boxes semisweet baking chocolate
1 (7 ounce) jar marshmallow creme
1 teaspoon vanilla extract
4 tablespoons unsalted butter
2 cups whole or chopped macadamia nuts
1 (12 ounce) can evaporated milk
4-1/2 cups granulated sugar

1. Generously grease a 13 x 9-inch baking dish (preferably glass) with 2 tablespoons butter. Set aside.

2. Place chocolate, marshmallow creme, vanilla, 4 tablespoons butter, and nuts in a large heatproof mixing bowl.

3. Combine milk and sugar in a large saucepan over medium-high heat. Bring to a boil, stirring occasionally to help sugar dissolve. When mixture boils, turn heat to low and cook for 6 minutes. Mixture will expand in pan, but DO NOT STIR. Remove pan from heat.

4. Immediately and carefully pour the heated mixture into the chocolate mixture. Begin stirring and continue until chocolate has melted and all ingredients are well blended. (You'll know this when stirring does not produce any dark chocolate "streaks" indicating unmelted chocolate.)

5. Pour into prepared dish. Smooth mixture with a knife or metal spoon back.

   Cut into squares after fudge has cooled. If you just can't wait, refrigerate for an hour or until fudge is firm enough to cut.

Package in a fabric covered box. Line with waxed tissue paper so that the box can be used later. Tie with a piece of lace and a sprig of dried herbs or flowers.

Whole Grain Jam Squares

Makes 28 squares

Yum, yum, yum...what a pleasant way to enjoy a cup of coffee or tea. Use different flavors of fruit spread for variety (my favorite is boysenberry).

1/2 pound unsalted butter, at room temperature
1 cup firmly packed brown sugar
1-3/4 cups all-purpose flour, white or wheat
1 teaspoon ground cinnamon
3/4 teaspoon salt
1/2 teaspoon baking soda
2 cups old-fashioned or quick cooking oats, uncooked
1 cup chopped walnuts
1 (16 ounce) jar fruit spread

1. Preheat oven to 400°F. Generously spray a 13 x 9-inch baking dish with no-stick cooking spray. Set aside.

2. Combine butter, sugar, flour, cinnamon, salt, soda, oatmeal, and walnuts in a large bowl. Mix well. Reserve 2 cups, and press the remaining mixture into prepared dish.

3. Smooth fruit spread evenly over mixture (see note). Crumble the remaining 2 cups of oatmeal mixture over fruit spread.

4. Bake 20 to 25 minutes. Cool completely before cutting into squares.

Note: *To make the fruit easier to spread, microwave on high (with the lid removed) in 20 second intervals. Stir and repeat if not spreadable. Be careful not to liquefy the spread.*

Stack squares on a serving plate. Make sure you've got them tightly wrapped or the gift may end up lighter than it starts out.

Lot'sa Cooking

These are recipes that I just couldn't leave out. They require at least two cooking steps, but don't let this stop you from trying every single one of them!

Dips & Doodles:
　Easy Stuffed Mushroom Caps
　Marinated Artichoke Squares
　Spiced Nuts
　Spiced Whole Almonds

Over the Top:
　The Best Homemade Croutons

On the Side:
　About Casserole Side Dishes
　- Calico Beans
　- Potatoes Romanoff
　- Simply, Rice Dish
　Six Week Bran Muffins

Finales:
　Killer Brownies
　Lemon Squares
　Mrs. Ward's Tropical Oatmeal Delights
　Easy Peach Upside-Down Cake
　Green Pudding Cake
　"Kitty Litter" Cake

Easy Stuffed Mushroom Caps

Serves 8 to 12

Your guests will be surprised to hear the ingredients of this flavorful stuffing. The mushrooms may be stuffed a day ahead of time. Cover them tightly and refrigerate until time to bake.

12 ounces mild or hot Italian sausage
1 pound fresh whole mushrooms
1 (8 ounce) package cream cheese, at room temperature
1/4 cup chopped fresh dill, for garnish

1. Preheat oven to 450°F. Crumble sausage into a skillet and cook slowly until well done. Remove sausage and drain on paper towels.

2. While sausage is cooking, remove dirt from the mushrooms with a "mushroom brush" (or <u>quickly</u> run them under water and dry immediately). Remove stems from mushrooms. Save stems for salads or finely chop and add to stuffing mix.

3. Combine sausage, chopped mushroom stems, and cream cheese, stirring until well mixed. Fill mushroom caps with sausage mixture. Bake for 30 minutes or until mushrooms are soft and cheese mixture is melted.

   Sprinkle with dill and serve immediately.

   Note: *Sausage may be cooked in advance. Refrigerate or freeze until ready to make the stuffing mixture.*

Fill a bucket or flower pot with fresh whole mushrooms. Nestle a small crock, bucket or flower pot filled with the stuffing mix in the mushrooms. Include a "mushroom brush" for cleaning and baking instructions.

Marinated Artichoke Squares

Makes about 6 dozen squares

These are "scrump-didily-icious". The best part...they're great hot or cold. The finished product may be frozen and re-heated to serve; wrap tightly in foil and place in a preheated 325°F oven for about 10 minutes.

2 (6-1/2 ounce) jars marinated artichoke hearts
1 medium onion, minced
1 garlic clove, minced
4 eggs, lightly beaten
1/3 cup dry bread crumbs
1/2 teaspoon dried oregano
1/2 teaspoon freshly ground black pepper
1/4 teaspoon salt
1/4 teaspoon Tabasco sauce
1/2 pound sharp Cheddar cheese, shredded
1/4 cup finely chopped Italian flat-leaf parsley

1. Preheat oven to 325°F. Spray an 11 x 7 x 2-inch baking dish with no-stick cooking spray. Set aside.

2. Place marinade from one jar of artichokes in skillet. Sauté onion and garlic until onion is transparent, about 5 minutes. Set aside.

3. Drain and finely chop artichokes. Set aside.

4. Combine eggs, bread crumbs, oregano, pepper, salt, and Tabasco in a medium bowl. Stir in artichokes, cheese, and parsley. Spread mixture into prepared pan.

5. Bake for 30 minutes or until mixture is firm in the center. Cool for 20 minutes. Cut into 1-inch squares.

Serve warm or at room temperature.

When the gift requested is an oblong baking dish, this is the filler! After baking, cover tightly and refrigerate until time to give. To complete the gift, tie on a garlic press or wooden utensil.

Spiced Nuts

Makes about 3 cups

Spiced nuts tend to be "overdone", but take on a new personality when cashews or hazelnuts are used.

1/2 cup granulated sugar
1/4 cup cornstarch
1/8 teaspoon salt
1-1/2 teaspoons ground cinnamon
1/2 teaspoon allspice
1/2 teaspoon nutmeg
1/3 teaspoon ground ginger
1 egg white
2 tablespoons cold water
1 pound whole cashews or hazelnuts

1. Preheat oven to 250°F. Line a baking sheet with aluminum foil. Spray foil generously with no-stick cooking spray.

2. Combine sugar, cornstarch, salt, cinnamon, allspice, nutmeg, and ginger in a mixing bowl. Set aside.

3. In a separate bowl, slightly beat the egg white and water. Place nuts in the egg mixture and drop one at a time in the sugar mixture; roll to coat well. Place coated nuts on prepared baking sheet.

4. Bake about 1-1/2 hours, stirring every 20 to 30 minutes. Cool nuts on baking sheet. Store in an airtight container.

Gift Giving

Fill a decorative tin with nuts and tuck into a basket of assorted treats.

Spiced Whole Almonds

Makes 6 cups

Coriander is the secret flavor in this addictive recipe. If you feel like splurging for a special friend, substitute macadamia nuts.

3/4 cup granulated sugar
2 tablespoons ground cinnamon
1 tablespoon ground coriander
3/4 teaspoon ground cloves
3 egg whites
zest of 1 orange
6 cups (about 2 pounds) whole raw almonds

1. Preheat oven to 275°F. Line two baking sheets with aluminum foil. Generously spray foil with no-stick cooking spray. Set aside.

2. Combine sugar, cinnamon, coriander, and cloves in a small mixing bowl. Set aside.

3. Beat egg whites until frothy. Stir in sugar mixture and orange zest. Add almonds. Stir until the nuts are evenly coated.

4. Spread half of the nuts in a single layer on each of the baking sheets. Bake on the center rack of the oven for 40 to 50 minutes, stirring every 10 minutes. Remove from oven and let cool on baking sheets for 1 hour. Store in an airtight container.

Gift Giving

Package in a glass container to show off the golden brown coating. Use anything from a canning jar to a crystal candy dish. Decorate the canning jar with colored raffia, garnish the candy dish with a bow of eyelet or lace.

The Best
Homemade Croutons
Makes 3 to 4 cups

Oh yeah! Once you've tasted these, packaged croutons just won't find their way into your home.

**1/2 large loaf over-one-day-old unsliced French
   sourdough bread**
1/2 pound salted or unsalted butter
**2 to 4 tablespoons regular or flavored extra virgin
   olive oil (I like basil)**
2 to 5 garlic cloves, peeled

1. Preheat oven to 350°F. Slice bread into 3/4 to 1-inch square cubes. Place butter and olive oil on a baking sheet with turned-up sides. Mince garlic cloves and place on top of unmelted butter.

2. Place baking sheet in oven and melt the butter. When almost melted, remove and add bread cubes. Stir well to coat cubes. Bake about 30 minutes or until golden brown, stirring every 10 minutes for even cooking. (Adjust cooking time based on the size of the bread cubes.)

3. Let croutons cool completely on the baking sheet before tasting. Two things will happen: the croutons will be crispier and you will not burn your mouth on the hot butter in the middle!

Gift Giving

The perfect filler for a Chinese food "take-out" container. If you can't locate colored containers, decorate white ones with colored markers, crayons, or whatever your imagination conjures up.

About Casserole Side Dishes

Casserole dishes are great gifts. They come in all shapes, sizes, colors, and finishes and can add a variety of looks to the food served in them. Alone, they look so empty, but adorned with goodies, they look so attractive!

Fill the empty dish with all of the recipe ingredients. Don't forget to include the recipe! Wrap with clear or colored cellophane, add a kitchen goodie or two, and there you have it!

Calico Beans

Serves 8 to 10

Beans, beans, and more beans...these are packed full of flavor, flavor, and more flavor. A perfect accompaniment to any meal or barbecue.

1/2 pound bacon
2 to 3 brown or red onions, thinly sliced
3/4 cup firmly packed brown sugar
1/2 cup ketchup
1/4 cup apple cider vinegar
1/4 teaspoon garlic salt
1/4 teaspoon dry mustard
1 (16 ounce) can pork and beans
1 (15 ounce) can large butter beans
1 (15-1/4 ounce) can green baby limas, drained
1 (15 ounce) can dark red kidney beans

1. Preheat oven to 350°F. Cut bacon into 1-inch pieces. Fry over medium-high heat until crisp. Remove bacon and drain on paper towels. Pour off all but 3 tablespoons bacon fat and stir in onions, brown sugar, ketchup, vinegar, garlic salt, and dry mustard. Stir and simmer, uncovered, for 20 minutes.

2. Combine beans, onion mixture, and 1/2 the bacon in a 3-quart covered casserole. Top with remaining bacon. Cover and bake 4 to 5 hours. Remove cover for the last 30 minutes.

Crock Pot Preparation: Beans need to be cooked for at least 12 hours. Start the night before or early in the morning. Prepare bacon and onion mixture as written. Substitute the crock pot for the covered casserole dish. Remove cover for the last two hours.

Enjoy the reactions when you give this gift. Include all of the ingredients (with the cooked bacon on top) along with a crock pot or bean pot. Stuff the ingredients in the container and place the remainder in a decorative gift bag. Stick some kitchen utensils out of the pot and gift bag, add some bows, and you could use this as a centerpiece!

Potatoes Romanoff

Serves 4 to 6

This is one of those dishes that everyone loves...reduced fat cheese and sour cream are acceptable, but non-fat cheese and sour cream will make this dish watery and lacking in flavor.

4 medium russet potatoes
1 cup sour cream
4 green onions, sliced
3/4 cup shredded sharp Cheddar cheese
1 teaspoon salt
1/8 teaspoon black pepper

Topping:
1/2 cup shredded sharp Cheddar cheese
paprika

1. Preheat oven to 350°F. Spray a 1-1/2 quart casserole with no-stick cooking spray. Set aside.

2. Cook potatoes in skin until tender (see note). Peel, if desired. Slice into 1/4-inch thick pieces. (It's okay if the pieces crumble.) Place potato pieces into a large bowl.

3. Combine potatoes, sour cream, onions, 3/4 cup cheese, salt, and pepper. Turn into prepared dish. Top with remaining 1/2 cup cheese and sprinkle with paprika.

4. Bake uncovered for 30 to 40 minutes until cheese is golden and potatoes are hot.

Note: *I prefer boiling the potatoes in water. This takes about 30 to 45 minutes for a fork to easily be inserted into the potato. If you're in a hurry, cook two at a time in the microwave for five minutes. Check for doneness and continue cooking at two minute intervals until tender. Repeat with the rest of the potatoes.*

Prepare the ingredients and place in prepared dish. Cover and include baking instructions. Attach a small basket with shakers of salt, pepper, and paprika.

Simply, Rice Dish

Serves 6 to 8

I have yet to meet someone who doesn't love this dish. The flavors blend so well, that additional seasoning is not needed.

2 cups cooked white rice
1 (4 ounce or 7 ounce) can diced green chiles
1/2 pound Cheddar cheese, shredded
3 cups sour cream

1. Preheat oven to 350°F. Spray a 1-1/2 quart casserole dish with no-stick cooking spray.

2. Using one-half of each ingredient, layer as follows: rice, chiles, cheese, sour cream. Repeat layers with the remaining ingredients, spreading the sour cream out to the edge of the dish.

3. Bake, uncovered, for 1 hour or until slightly browned.

    Note: *This dish may be made up to a day in advance, just cover and refrigerate. For even cooking, allow the casserole to come to room temperature before baking.*

With only four ingredients, this gift can look pretty plain in the casserole dish. Wrap each ingredient with fabric remnants. Use rick-rack or lace for bows. Add the recipe and you're done!

Six Week Bran Muffins

Makes 18 to 24 muffins

This recipe allows you to have fresh-baked muffins daily, if you wish.
Remember to keep the uncooked batter in a tightly sealed container.

5-1/2 cups raisin bran cereal
3 cups granulated sugar
5 cups all-purpose flour
5 teaspoons baking soda
2 teaspoons salt
1 quart buttermilk
1 cup canola oil
4 eggs, beaten

1. Combine cereal, sugar, flour, soda, and salt in a large bowl. Set aside.

2. Combine buttermilk, oil, and eggs in a medium bowl. Add to cereal mixture. Stir by hand until all ingredients have incorporated.

3. Bake or cover tightly and refrigerate up to 6 weeks.

   Baking Instructions: Preheat oven to 400˚F. Fill muffin cups to the top. Bake for 18 to 23 minutes. Remove from oven and let stand 5 minutes. Remove muffins from pan and place on a cooling rack.

Gift Giving

Wrap each muffin with colored plastic wrap. Place wrapped muffins in the cups of a new muffin pan. Include the remainder of the batter in a container with a tight fitting lid and the baking instructions.

Killer Brownies

Serves 18 to 24

I started out calling these "Chocolate Chip Brownies", but they were quickly renamed at a summer potluck. These are a to-die-for treat, especially when topped with your favorite ice cream and topping sauce. Casual enough for a backyard barbecue, yet elegant enough for a sit-down dinner.

1 package chocolate cake mix
1 (4 serving size) package chocolate instant pudding
1/4 cup canola oil
1 (16 ounce) package semisweet chocolate chips

In addition to the ingredients listed above, you will need to purchase the ingredients listed on the cake mix.

1. Spray a 13 x 9-inch or 15 x 10-inch rectangular pan with no-stick cooking spray. Preheat oven according to instructions on the cake mix package.

2. Combine the dry cake mix and dry pudding in a large mixing bowl. Add the ingredients called for on the cake mix package plus the 1/4 cup oil. Mix according to the cake mix package instructions. Stir in chocolate chips.

3. Pour into prepared baking pan. Bake according to the instructions on the cake mix package. Cool completely before serving.

Gift Giving

Cut into serving pieces and arrange on a wooden platter. Include an ice cream serving scoop and your favorite flavor of ice cream topping sauce. The recipient of the gift will definitely get the idea!

Lemon Squares

Makes about 2 dozen squares

Tart, tangy, sweet, easy....what more could you ask for?

8 tablespoons unsalted butter, at room temperature
1 cup all-purpose flour
1/4 cup powdered sugar
2 eggs
1 cup granulated sugar
1/4 cup fresh lemon juice

Topping:
1/4 to 1/2 cup powdered sugar

1. Preheat oven to 350°F. Spray an 11 x 7-inch rectangular baking dish with no-stick cooking spray. Set aside.

2. Combine butter, flour, and powdered sugar in a medium bowl. Press the mixture into the prepared baking dish.

3. Combine eggs, granulated sugar, and lemon juice in a small bowl. Pour over flour mixture.

4. Bake for 25 minutes. Remove from oven and sift powdered sugar over the warm lemon squares. (Sifting may be done by placing the powdered sugar in a mesh strainer. Gently shake the strainer over the dish.) Allow to cool before cutting into squares. Store in an airtight container.

These are elegant presented on a paper doily on a clear glass plate. Wrap with cellophane.

Mrs. Ward's Tropical Oatmeal Delights

Makes 5 dozen

There never seem to be enough of these to go around. These cookies are dedicated to all of my Moloka'i friends, where this recipe was born.

**1-1/2 cups all-purpose flour
1 teaspoon baking soda
1 teaspoon ground cinnamon
1/2 teaspoon salt
3 cups old-fashioned oats, uncooked
1 cup dried tropical fruit mix*
1 cup roasted, unsalted macadamia nuts
1/2 pound unsalted butter, at room temperature
1 cup firmly packed brown sugar
1/2 cup granulated sugar
2 eggs
1 teaspoon vanilla extract**

* Make your own fruit mix with diced pieces of dried pineapple, mango, papaya, and raisins.

1. Preheat oven to 350°F.

2. Combine flour, baking soda, cinnamon and salt in a bowl. Set aside. In another bowl, combine oats, fruit, and nuts. Set aside.

3. Beat butter and sugars until creamy. Add eggs and vanilla and continue beating until well combined. Add flour mixture and stir well. Add oat mixture. Stir by hand until all ingredients are evenly mixed.

4. Place on baking sheets with a cookie scoop, or drop by tablespoon. Bake 10 to 12 minutes, or until the edges are golden brown. For even baking, turn the baking sheet one-half turn after half of the baking time has elapsed.

5. Cool cookies on baking sheet for 5 minutes before transferring to cooling racks.

Note: *A cookie scoop produces a more uniform-sized cookie.*

Stack the cookies in cellophane bags or candy boxes. Attach an ice cream serving scoop and suggest creating your own ice cream sandwiches.

Easy Peach Upside-Down Cake

Serves 10 to 12

Try this for a change from the traditional Pineapple Upside-Down Cake.

1 package yellow cake mix
8 tablespoons unsalted butter
1 cup firmly packed brown sugar
1 (15 ounce) can peach slices, drained
maraschino cherries, drained and cut into halves

In addition to the ingredients listed above, you will need to purchase the ingredients listed on the cake mix.

1. Preheat oven to 350°F or the appropriate temperature for the size of pan you're using as listed on the cake mix box.

2. Prepare the cake batter according to the directions on the box; set aside.

3. Melt butter and brown sugar in the oven in the baking pan. Place peaches and cherries over the melted butter in the pattern of your choice. Pour prepared cake batter over fruit being careful not let batter displace the fruit.

4. Bake cake according to the directions on the box. When cake is done, immediately invert onto a serving dish.

Gift Giving

Include the cake when the gift is a serving platter. A cake server is a great compliment to the gift.

Green Pudding Cake

Serves 12 to 16

This has become a St. Patrick's Day tradition, although I do serve it all year long. It's one of the few desserts that our dessert-disliking friend, Chris, will eat.

1 (4 serving size) package pistachio instant pudding
1 package yellow cake mix (without pudding in mix)
1/2 teaspoon almond extract
4 eggs
1-1/4 cups water
1/4 cup canola oil
7 drops green food coloring (optional)

Topping:
1/4 to 1/2 cup powdered sugar

1. Preheat oven to 350°F. Spray a 13 x 9-inch baking pan or Bundt pan with no-stick cooking spray.

2. Combine all ingredients in a large bowl. With an electric mixer, beat for 4 minutes on medium speed.

3. Pour the batter into the prepared pan and bake as follows:
13 x 9-inch pan	40 to 50 minutes	350°F
Bundt pan	45 to 50 minutes	350°F

4. Cool the cake in the pan for about 15 minutes. Invert on a serving platter and sprinkle with powdered sugar.

Gift Giving

Give a Bundt pan with all the ingredients tucked into the pan, wrap with cellophane and tie a bag of pistachio nuts on the outside!

"Kitty Litter" Cake

Serves 20 to 24

What a name for such a delicious dessert. This won first place in a dessert contest for my best bud's in-laws, Jack & Betty. First place just happened to be a one week, all expense paid trip for two to the Bahamas!!

**1 new medium to large kitty litter box
    (without odor control)**
1 new kitty litter shovel
1 package spice cake mix
1 package white cake mix
**1 (4 serving size) package vanilla pudding,
    regular or instant**
**1/2 pound vanilla sandwich cookies, crumbled
    in a food processor**
4 to 12 drops green food coloring
1 to 2 tablespoons water
12 small Tootsie Rolls

In addition to the ingredients listed above, you will need to purchase the ingredients listed on the cake mixes and the pudding mix.

1. Prepare and bake cakes according to the package instructions. The size of the pan does not matter as the cakes will be broken up. Let the cakes cool completely.

2. While cakes are baking, make the pudding according to the package instructions. Chill in the refrigerator.

3. Mix 1/4 cup of the crumbled cookies with several drops of green food coloring diluted in a tablespoon or two of water. Stir to distribute the food coloring. Set aside.

Note: *These steps may be done the day before.*

4. When cakes are completely cool, break them into a crumbly texture in a large mixing bowl. Add remaining cookie crumbs (not the green ones). Add pudding and gently stir. Keep the mixture as light and fluffy as possible.

5. To assemble the finished product: line the litter box with plastic wrap, waxed paper, aluminum foil, or parchment paper. Pour the cake mixture into the box and smooth it out, but do not "smush" it flat.

6. Place Tootsie Rolls (3 to 4 at a time) on a plate in the microwave for 10 to 20 seconds. When soft and pliable, mold them to look like pieces of kitty "doo-doo". Place in the cake litter. Sprinkle the green cookie crumbs over top of cake. Serve with the "pooper scooper".

Gift Giving

Along with the cake-filled litter box and "pooper scooper", include personalized pet bowls for your guests. Give the dish to each guest as a remembrance.

The End Stuff

Glossary

al dente: describes the doneness of food (usually pasta) that offers a slight resistance when bitten into. The food is not soft or overdone.

allspice berries: a small brown berry from the pimento tree. The flavor tastes like a combination of cinnamon, clove, nutmeg, ginger, and pepper.

aquavit; akvavit: a Scandinavian alcoholic distilled beverage flavored with caraway seeds.

baking sheet: a firm, flat sheet of metal for baking cookies and biscuits. Some have turned-up sides.

balsamic vinegar: a dark, aromatic Italian vinegar with a sweet-sour flavor. It is made from fermented grape juice and aged in wooden casks.

Calvados: an apple brandy made in Calvados, Normandy, France.

cardamom: an intensely aromatic spice from the ginger family. The seed has a strong, lemony flavor, but do not attempt to substitute anything for this spice.

chili sauce: a flavorful sauce (usually with "a kick") made from tomatoes, chiles, green peppers, onions, vinegar, sugar, and spices.

Chinese black beans: small black soybeans preserved in salt (also known as "fermented black beans"). They are very salty, with a strong flavor and are most commonly used in Chinese cuisine.

chop: to cut food into small pieces of varying sizes.

cilantro: also known as "Chinese parsley" or "coriander leaves". The leaves are a dark, lacy green and resemble Italian flat-leaf parsley. This fresh herb is widely used in Asian, Caribbean, and Latin American cooking.

combine: to mix two or more ingredients together until they do not separate.

compote: fresh or dried fruit slowly cooked in a sugar syrup. Liquor and/or spices may be added.

coriander: the tiny yellow-tan seeds of the cilantro plant. Whole seeds are used for pickling and mulling spices. Ground seeds are most commonly used in baked goods and soups.

dice: to cut food into equal-size cubes, 1/4 to 5/8-inch.

Dijon mustard: a mustard of yellow-gray color, medium-hot flavor, and creamy texture. Originally made in the Dijon region of France.

emulsify: a mixture of two unmixable liquids, such as oil and vinegar.

fold: to incorporate light, airy ingredients into heavier ingredients by gently moving them from the bottom up and over the top in a circular motion without stirring or beating.

frothy: a mixture that has a formation of tiny, light bubbles.

Galliano: a yellow-orange, anise-flavored liqueur from Italy.

garlic press: a tool used to force garlic cloves through small holes to make a paste.

ginger; ginger root: the gnarled, bumpy root of the ginger plant. It is spicy with a strong aroma, yet has a slightly sweet flavor. Available fresh, powdered, preserved in sugar, crystallized, candied, or pickled.

grate: to reduce food to small pieces by scraping it on one of the surfaces of a "grater" or other rough surface.

hoisin sauce: a thick, reddish-brown, sweet (and sometimes spicy) sauce made from soybeans, garlic, chile peppers, and spices. Available in Asian markets and large supermarkets.

hot pepper oil: olive oil infused with the flavor of chile peppers. Available in Asian markets and large supermarkets.

hummus: a thick Middle Eastern sauce made from mashed chickpeas (also called garbanzo beans) seasoned with lemon juice, garlic, and olive or sesame oil.

infusion: a hot liquid that has had food or seasoning steeped in it until the liquid absorbs the flavor.

Italian flat-leaf parsley: a variety of parsley that is more strongly flavored than the curly-leaf variety. Sold in bunches and available in most supermarket produce departments.

Jalapeño chile: a short, green, tapered Mexican chile with smooth dark skin. It is moderately hot to very hot and, when allowed to ripen, turns red.

jícama: a brown-skinned bulbous root vegetable with white crunchy flesh, eaten raw or cooked. Peel before using flesh.

julienne: food cut into matchstick shapes of 1/8 by 1/8 by 1/2-inch. Length may be longer, if desired.

juniper berry: the dried blue-black berry of an evergreen bush. They are aromatic as well as bitter.

Kahlúa: a coffee-flavored liqueur made in Mexico.

Kosher salt: purified coarse rock salt.

liqueur: a strong, sweet alcoholic beverage made from a distilled spirit base sweetened, flavored, and colored with fruits and aromatics.

mince: to cut or chop food into fine pieces.

opal basil: a variety of basil that has a purple-colored leaf, sometimes ruffled.

pasta water: water that is left after the pasta has been cooked.

pequin chile: a small dried red-orange chile with a sweet, smokey flavor.

pesto: an uncooked sauce made from fresh basil, garlic, olive oil, pine nuts, and Parmesan cheese.

pesto paste: pesto with a paste-like texture. This allows the user to thin the pesto to a desired consistency with water from cooked pasta, olive oil, or other liquid.

pimiento: a large, heart-shaped sweet pepper with red skin. Available canned and bottled.

pine nut: an ivory-colored nut, with rich flavor from various pine trees. Also known as pinon, pignoli, and pignolia.

pocket bread: also known as pita bread. A Middle Eastern round, flat bread that is split open or cut cross-wise to form a pocket and filled with a stuffing. Available in Middle Eastern markets and most supermarkets.

purée: to process food by mashing, straining, or fine chopping to form a smooth pulp.

ramekin: a small, ceramic soufflé dish with a 4-ounce capacity.

Roma tomato: an oval-shaped, flavorful, meaty tomato in red and yellow varieties. Also known as the plum tomato or Italian plum.

rotini: spaghetti in the shape of spirals.

sauté: a dry-heat cooking method over high heat that transfers heat from the pan to the food with a small amount of cooking oil.

sea salt: salt recovered by the evaporation of seawater.

sesame oil: an oil obtained from the sesame seed. It has a rich, nutty flavor. The dark, Asian variety should be used in small amounts.

shallot: a member of the onion family formed like garlic with a head composed of several cloves. The flavor more subtle than an onion and not as bold as garlic.

shred: to reduce food to long narrow strips by grating or cutting.

soufflé dish: a round, ovenproof, porcelain baking dish with straight sides and a smooth interior.

sun-dried tomatoes: tomatoes dried in the sun to produce a chewy, intensely flavored, dark ruby red tomato. Available dried or packed in olive oil.

sweet potato: a starchy tuber from the morning glory plant. Unrelated to the potato and yam, flavor is sweet. Skin colors vary from light yellow to dark orange.

tepid: lukewarm. Usually refers to the temperature of water.

tomatillo: a fruit that resembles a small tomato with a papery husk which is removed before using the fruit. The bright green skin protects the tart interior flesh. Available in Latin American markets as well as larger supermarkets and specialty produce stores.

torte: a rich cake, made with ground nuts or bread crumbs instead of flour. They may be multilayered and filled with jams, whipped cream, or buttercream.

turmeric: a dried, powdery spice from the root of a tropical plant related to ginger. Flavor is strong and spicy. Color is an intense yellow-orange. Very popular in East Indian cooking.

unsalted butter: simply, butter that contains no salt. I prefer this unseasoned product for baking.

vinaigrette: an emulsion of oil and vinegar primarily used as a salad dressing. Season with herbs, spices, salt, and pepper.

whisk: a utensil consisting of several loops of wires joined at a handle to form a teardrop shape. Used to incorporate air into foods such as eggs, cream, and sauces.

yam: a thick, tropical vine tuber. Unrelated to potatoes and sweet potatoes, yams contain more natural sugar and have a higher moisture content, yet are not as sweet as a sweet potato. Skin color ranges from off-white to dark brown; flesh may be a creamy white to a deep red.

zest: the colored outermost skin of citrus fruits. The oils in the zest add flavor to the food.

Mail Order Sources

There are numerous sources for obtaining foods and items to use for gift giving. Shopping by mail can simplify your life by letting you shop when it's convenient for you, but don't forget to support your community stores and businesses.

Here are some sources to try:

The Chile Shop, Inc.
109 East Water Street
Santa Fe, NM 87501
505/983-6080 fax: 505/984-0737
store and catalogue
dried chiles & chile powders, giftware

Embellishments
P.O. Box 1506
Cleveland, MS 38732
Toll Free 1-800-600-6885
catalogue
gift packaging for personal gifts of food

Penzeys, Ltd.
P.O. Box 933
Muskego, WI 53150
414/679-7207 fax: 414/679-7878
catalogue
spices and seasonings

Purdy's Natural Macadamia Nuts
Na Hua 'O Ka Aina
P.O. Box 84
Ho'olehua, Molokai, Hawaii 96729
mail order
macadamia nuts,
raw and roasted (no salt or oil added)

Index